Globalisation Laid Bare

Lessons in International Business

Sir Richard Branson
Introduction

GIBSON SQUARE
London

First edition published in the UK by

UK Tel: +44 (0)20 7096 1100
    Fax: +44 (0)20 7993 2214

US Tel: +1 646 216 9813
    Fax: +1 646 216 9488

Eire Tel: +353 (0)1 657 1057

info@gibsonsquare.com
www.gibsonsquare.com

ISBN 9 7 8 1 9 0 6 1 4 2 1 9 3

All rights reserved. No part of this publication may be reproduced, stored in a retrieval system, or transmitted, in any form or by any means, electronic, mechanical, photocopying, recording or otherwise without the prior consent of the publisher. A catalogue record for this book is available from the Library of Congress and the British Library. Copyright © 2009 by The Industry and Parliament Trust.

CONTENTS

Acknowledgements
Prefacee
Contributor Biographies

Richard Branson
   Introduction   37

Alan Greenspan
   A Cushion against Risk   43
Amartya Sen
   Adam Smith never Stood Alone   51

1 Subi Rangan
   Globalisation the JEDI Way   59
2 Vincent Cable
   The UK's Role in the World Economy   71

3 Harold Chee
   Investing in the UK versus Investing in China   87
4 Jim O'Neill
   BRICs and Mortar   99
5 Clare Short
   Globalisation: Fostering Inequality and Poverty?   119
6 Vandana Shiva
   The Social Costs of Economic Globalisation   131
7 Peter Jones
   Globalisation and SMEs   143
8 Stuart Rose
   Business and Sustainability   151
9 Chris Tuppen
   Corporate Responsibility and Competitiveness   163
10 Jeffrey Owen
   Providing a Global Tax Environment   173
11 Alan Duncan
   Soft Power and Aggressive Investment   179
12 Peter Mandelson
   Demographic Change, Globalisation and Trade Policy 189

Notes

ACKNOWLEDGEMENTS

In 2006 an Industry and Parliament Trust colleague, Sharon Bray, brought to my attention her idea of an Industry and Parliament Trust (IPT) publication. After some deliberation the topic of globalisation was agreed upon and members of the business community, academics and parliamentarians were approached to write a series of essays looking at various aspects of globalisation.

This collection of essays reflects the ethos and mission of the IPT to build a bridge between the worlds of those who create wealth and those who legislate. It has brought together business leaders and politicians to write on the important and engaging issues surrounding globalisation. The publication of such a collection in this current economic climate is now more topical than ever.

I would like to thank Amelia Knott, Amy Whitelock, Will White and Matt Muir who were highly supportive in proof reading and the necessary updating of the essays.

I would also like to thank Sheila Palmer for her skilled administrative support and the IPT Chairman and Board of Trustees for their ongoing encouragement.

Sarah Hutchison
Chief Operating Officer
Industry and Parliament Trust
May 2009

PREFACE

The idea to publish a book on the subject of globalisation was first mooted within the Industry and Parliament Trust, three years ago. Members of the business community, academics and parliamentarians were approached and invited to contribute essays looking at various aspects of doing business in a world that has been made smaller through faster communications and the ease of international travel.

The current economic crisis, acknowledged to have extensive global dimensions and causes makes publication of this book topical and even more essential reading than could have been anticipated.

I would like to personally thank all the contributors for taking the time to put their thoughts to paper and particularly to Sarah Hutchison, a senior executive of the Industry and Parliament Trust for so successfully managing the project.

Lastly, thanks are due to Richard Branson for

introducing this book. Virgin Atlantic has provided vital support to the Industry and Parliament Trust's International programmes, allowing parliamentarians the opportunity to leave Westminster and learn more at first hand about the operation of the global economy.

Bill Olner MP
Chairman
Industry and Parliament Trust
May 2009

CONTRIBUTOR BIOGRAPHIES

Sir Richard Branson: I was born in 1950 and educated at Stowe School. It was here that I set up *Student* magazine when I was 16. In 1970 I founded Virgin as a mail order record retailer, and shortly afterwards I opened a record shop in Oxford Street, London. In 1972 we built a recording studio in Oxfordshire where the first Virgin artist, Mike Oldfield, recorded 'Tubular Bells'. In 1977 we signed the Sex Pistols and we went on to sign many household names from Culture Club to the Rolling Stones, helping to make Virgin Music one of the top six record companies in the world. With around 200 companies in over 30 countries, the Virgin Group has now expanded into leisure, travel, tourism, mobile, broadband, TV, radio, music festivals, finance and health and through Virgin Green Fund we are investing in renewable energy and resource efficiency. In February 2007, we announced the Virgin Earth Challenge—a $25 million prize to encourage a viable technology which will result in the net removal of anthropogenic, atmospheric greenhouse gases. In July of the same year I had the honour of joining my good friend Peter Gabriel, Nelson Mandela, Graça Machel, and Desmond Tutu to announce the formation of The Elders, a group of leaders to contribute their wisdom, independent leadership and integrity to tackle some of the world's toughest problems. I am also very proud of the work of Virgin Unite, our not-for-profit entrepreneurial foundation, which continues to focus on entrepreneurial approaches to social and environmental issues and enjoy supporting their work in every way I can.

Dr Vincent Cable MP graduated from Cambridge University, where he was President of the Union, followed by a PhD at Glasgow University. He has had a varied career which includes time at the Foreign Office, Chatham House and as Shell's Chief Economist. Vincent Cable was first elected to Parliament to represent Twickenham in 1997. He has been the Liberal Democrat Shadow Chancellor since November 2003 and is currently Deputy Leader of the Liberal Democrats. He has published several books and reports on international economics, trade and environmental issues.

Harold Chee is a senior tutor & client director at Ashridge Business School in the UK. His expertise is in Leadership, Cross Cultural Management & Chinese Business. His clients include Sinopec, China Post, etc. He works extensively in China, Europe and the USA and has several publications such as *The Myths of Doing Business in China* (2nd edition 2007, transl. into Italian and German), *Exporting Management Technology to Chinese*

Managers (Directions-Ashridge Journal 2002), *Global Marketing Strategies* (1998 *Financial Times*/Pitman), Currently he is co-authoring a book on Chinese Leadership with Wang Xiaoyu.

Alan Duncan MP has been a pivotal influence in the fortunes of the Conservative for well over ten years. It was his campaign skills which secured the election of William Hague as leader in 1997, following the resignation of John Major after seven years as Prime Minister. He has been at the forefront of efforts to modernise the party and to shift it from holding old-fashioned traditional social attitudes to becoming a party which is socially and economically liberal. He is one of the senior Conservatives who are realigning the party under David Cameron. Alan has held a series of posts in the Shadow Cabinet, including International Development, Constitutional Affairs, Transport and Trade & Industry (DBERR) and now as Shadow Leader of the House of Commons. A popular figure on TV and radio, he is a regular contributor to the BBC's 'Any Questions' and 'Question Time' and has appeared three times on 'Have I Got News For You?'. Alan was educated at Oxford University, where he read politics & economics, and was President of the Oxford Union, and then later as a Kennedy Scholar at Harvard. After an initial period with Shell, he spent over ten years as an oil trader with Marc Rich & Co, and has extensive experience both in the energy sector and with the oil-producing countries of the world. He is regarded as the Conservative Party's most informed pundit on the politics of the Middle East and is a regular traveller to the region. One of his closest friends for over 30 years was the murdered former

Prime Minister of Pakistan, Benazir Bhutto. Since 1992 he has been the MP for Rutland & Melton, a traditional rural area in the Midlands.

Dr Alan Greenspan was Chairman of the Board of Governors of the Federal Reserve System of the United States from 1987 to 2006.

Peter Jones: I founded Phones International Group in 1998, which has been recognised as one of the most successful UK businesses in recent years. My business interests now span many other areas than just telecommunications, including incentives and gifts, entertainment, publishing, property and television. At the end of 2006, *The Daily Telegraph* listed me as one of the top ten entrepreneurs in the UK aged under 40.

Lord Mandelson was appointed Secretary of State for Business, Enterprise & Regulatory Reform in 2008. He previously served as European Commissioner for Trade from 2004. Prior to that he was Member of Parliament for Hartlepool and served in the Cabinet as Trade and Industry Secretary and Northern Ireland Secretary.

Dr Jim O'Neill is Head of Global Economics, Commodities and Strategy Research for Goldman Sachs. In this role, Jim manages the firm's economics, strategy and commodity research and the output of these teams around the world. Jim received his PhD in 1982 from the University of Surrey after graduating in Economics from Sheffield University in 1978. After a brief spell with Bank of America and International Treasury Management, a division of Marine Midland Bank, in 1988 Jim joined

Swiss Bank Corporation (SBC). In 1991, he became Head of Research, globally, for SBC. Jim joined Goldman Sachs in October 1995 as a Partner, Co-Head of Global Economics Research and Chief Currency Economist, becoming Head of Global Economics Research in 2001. Jim is the creator of the acronym BRICs and, together with his colleagues, he has published much research about BRICs, which has become synonymous with the emergence of Brazil, Russia, India and China as the growth opportunities of the future. Jim is a member of the board of the Royal Economic Society in the UK, of the European think-tank Bruegel, and Itinera, a Belgium think-tank. He is a member of the UK-India Round Table, and the UKIBC. Jim is one of the founding trustees, as well as currently Chairman, of the London-based charity SHINE. He sits on the board of a number of other charities, primarily specialising in education. In 2009, Jim received an honorary doctorate from the Institute of Education, University of London, for his educational philanthropy. He also served as a non-executive director of Manchester United before it returned to private ownership in 2005.

Dr Jeffrey P. Owens is a public finance expert with a doctorate in Economics from Cambridge University in the United Kingdom. He is also trained as an accountant. He is the Director of the OECD's Centre for Tax Policy and Administration which is the focal point for the Organisation's work on taxation. Over the last ten years he has built up the OECD's work on taxation so that it is now the leading organisation in the international tax area. He has taught at Cambridge University, the American University in Paris, Bocconi University in Italy and

Queen Mary's College in London. He is a member of numerous scientific committees and frequently contributes to international conferences and journals.

Professor Subi Rangan received an MBA from the MIT Sloan School of Management and a PhD from Harvard University. His research and teaching interests revolve around the strategy and management challenges facing multinational firms. In 1998, Professor Rangan won the Academy of International Business' Eldridge Haynes Prize (awarded biennially to a scholar under forty) for the best original essay in international business. In 1995, that academy awarded their Best Dissertation Award to his doctoral thesis. His articles appear in such journals as *Academy of Management Review, Journal of International Business Studies, Strategic Management Journal,* and the *Sloan Management Review*. Professor Rangan is coauthor of two books: *Manager in the International Economy,* a 1996 Prentice-Hall text on international business; and *A Prism on Globalization,* Brookings Institution, 1999. He is working currently on the topics of global competition among and crossborder cooperation within multinational firms. He serves on the editorial boards of *Journal of International Business Studies, Journal of International Management,* and *Strategic Management Journal.* In 1998, Professor Rangan won the Outstanding Teacher award (and was nominated again in 1999, 2002, and 2003) for his MBA elective course on global strategy and management.

Sir Stuart Rose has worked in retail for over 30 years starting at Marks & Spencer plc in 1972 and joining the Burton Group in 1989. Following the Group's demerger in 1997 he became Chief Executive of Argos plc. In

1998 he became Chief Executive of Booker plc which was merged with the Iceland Group in 2000. He became Chief Executive of Arcadia Group plc in November 2000 and left in December 2002 following its acquisition. He was named Chief Executive of Marks & Spencer plc in May 2004 and became Chairman in 2008. He is Chairman of Business in the Community and a non-executive director of Land Securities plc. Stuart was knighted in 2008 for services to the retail industry and corporate social responsibility.

Professor Amartya Sen is Lamont University Professor, and Professor of Economics and Philosophy, at Harvard University and was until recently the Master of Trinity College, Cambridge. He has served as President of the Econometric Society, the Indian Economic Association, the American Economic Association and the International Economic Association. He was formerly Honorary President of OXFAM and is now its Honorary Advisor. Previously he was the Drummond Professor of Political Economy at Oxford University, and a Fellow of All Souls College, and is now a Distinguished Fellow of All Souls. Professor Sen received the Nobel Prize in Economics in 1998 for his contribution to welfare economics.

Born in India in 1952, *Dr Vandana Shiva* is a world-renowned environmental leader and thinker. Director of the Research Foundation on Science, Technology, and Ecology, she is the author of many books. Shiva is a leader in the International Forum on Globalization, along with Ralph Nader and Jeremy Rifkin. She addressed the World Trade Organization summit in

Seattle, 1999, as well as the World Economic Forum in Melbourne, 2000. In 1993, Shiva won the Alternative Nobel Peace Prize (the Right Livelihood Award). The founder of Navdanya ('nine seeds'), a movement promoting diversity and use of native seeds, she also set up the Research Foundation for Science, Technology, and Ecology in her mother's cowshed in 1997. Its studies have validated the ecological value of traditional farming and been instrumental in fighting destructive development projects in India. Before becoming an activist, Shiva was one of India's leading physicists. She holds a master's degree in the philosophy of science and a PhD in particle physics.

Of Irish ancestry, *Clare Short MP* was born in Birmingham and graduated from the Universities of Keele and Leeds as Bachelor of Arts with Honours in Political Science. She previously worked as a Civil Servant at the Home Office and entered the House of Commons in 1983 as the Member of Parliament for Birmingham Ladywood, which seat she has held since then, and is the area where she was born and grew up. In 2003, Ms Short resigned from the Government over the Iraq war and in 2006, she resigned the Labour whip. She now sits as an Independent. In 2004, Ms Short's book *An Honourable Deception? New Labour, Iraq, and the Misuse of Power* was published as an attempt to explain why Tony Blair did what he did on Iraq so that lessons could be learned and things put right. In 2005, it was awarded Political Book of the Year by Channel 4. Widowed with one son, she lists swimming and her family as her main leisure pursuits.

As Chief Sustainability Officer, *Chris Tuppen*'s remit

covers all aspects of British Telecom's approach to sustainability and corporate responsibility issues. In addition to helping set the company's sustainability strategy he is directly responsible for producing the company's corporate accountability report and frequently engages with strategic stakeholders including regulators, investors and customers. He was co-editor of the report *SMART 2020: Enabling the Low Carbon Economy in the Information Age* and in January 2008 he was named by a special *Guardian* newspaper panel of prominent environmental figures as one of the 50 people who could save the planet from climatic disaster.

INTRODUCTION

✺

RICHARD BRANSON

Few terms provoke like globalisation. Our perceptions of this phenomenon are dictated both by its process and by its consequences—consequences that are far from clear. Little wonder, therefore, that the topic engenders such passionate yet disparate views.

Globalisation is the process by which geographic constraints on economic, social and cultural arrangements recede, thus increasing our global interdependence. The effects of this process are being felt right across the political and commercial spectra. Issues stemming from globalisation make up some of the primary concerns for UK businesses, whilst being amongst the least understood by both politicians and wealth creators.[1] These include international competition, global trade, the rise of India and China and changes in capital and labour distribution. Education is therefore vital in order to achieve regulatory and business climates that are most conducive to our continued prosperity.

The Industry and Parliament Trust has been connecting the worlds of business and parliament for over thirty years. It aims to promote greater understanding and ethical, mutually beneficial relationships between Parliaments and the business community, leading to well informed policies and efficient administration for the public benefit. The Trust achieves these aims through educational services that inform parliamentarians about business operations, businesses about the legislative processes and civil servants about parliamentary procedures. In keeping with those aspirations, this book has brought together the significant expertise of a number of high profile figures from all sides of the spectrum to tackle some of the major issues surrounding globalisation.

Dr Alan Greenspan and Professor Amartya Sen provide their perspective on the 2008 turbulence in the international financial markets. Professor Subi Rangan introduces the subject and provides an original overview of the tensions that can arise between the worlds of business and politics in the face of untrammelled globalisation—and a potential solution in the form of 'JEDI' globalisation. The Rt Hon Dr Vince Cable MP then evaluates the UK's place in an increasingly globalised economy, and looks ahead to examine some of the challenges facing larger economies going forward. This provides the context for Harold Chee's timely comparison of investment opportunities in the UK and China, which argues for the mutual benefits of increased trade between the two. Dr Jim O'Neill, the originator of the BRIC[2] acronym, then analyses the growth potential of these fast developing economies over the coming quarter of a century.

Some less favourable consequences of globalisation are examined by the Rt Hon Clare Short MP, who evaluates the inequality and poverty often associated with the phenomenon and, crucially, what this means for its continuation. Dr Vandana Shiva's case study of Indian agriculture powerfully illustrates the social costs of globalisation and the huge challenge they represent. However, as our high streets reveal, the difficulties of managing globalisation at a local level are not unique to developing countries. Entrepreneur Peter Jones offers a frank outline of the challenges facing the UK's small and medium sized enterprises who wish to expand into global markets.

For many larger companies the opportunities created by globalisation have brought the potential for greater margins, but at an ethical cost. This is examined from the shop floor by Sir Stuart Rose, Chairman of Marks & Spencer, who gives an overview of the steps his company is taking to ensure ethical, sustainable, and yet still profitable, business in a global economy. The same subject is tackled by Chris Tuppen, Chief Sustainability Officer for BT group, who looks at the relationship between business and ethics in an increasingly globalised world and the steps that need to be taken to bring the two into line.

Dr Jeffrey Owens, Director of the OECD's Centre for Tax Policy, looks at five decades of bilateral tax treaties, and their importance in creating fair, equitable and above all stable trading environments in the troubled financial times we are facing. This is particularly important given the review that follows in which Alan Duncan MP examines how the cash reserves and trading capacity of the global economy's rising powers have altered the geopolitical landscape. Trading routes and relationships are changing beyond recognition, forcing analysts to redraw traditional spheres of influence. Globalisation has also affected global demographics, bringing its own impacts upon business and politics as Lord Mandelson, former European Commissioner and current Secretary of State and

Government Spokesperson for Business, Enterprise and Regulatory Reform demonstrates, closing the collection with the observation that, despite the risks and difficulties here outlined, globalisation is essential for continued economic growth.

These fourteen distinguished contributors, who have given their time so generously, have in just a few pages explored and illuminated many of the major issues facing the UK and the world today. I fail to see how anyone involved in the spheres of business or politics would not benefit from reading these highly informative, interesting and accessible essays. Parliamentarians will be better legislators and companies more thoughtful in their business dealings thanks to this insightful collection.

A CUSHION AGAINST RISK

regulators can set and enforce
capital and collateral requirements
but they cannot predict the future

✸

ALAN GREENSPAN

The extraordinary risk-management discipline that developed out of the writings of the University of Chicago's Harry Markowitz in the 1950s produced insights that won several Nobel prizes in economics. It was widely embraced not only by academia but also by a large majority of financial professionals and global regulators.

But in August 2007, the risk-management structure cracked. All the sophisticated mathematics and computer wizardry essentially rested on one central premise: that the enlightened self-interest of owners and managers of financial institutions would lead them to maintain a sufficient buffer against insolvency by actively monitoring their firms' capital and risk positions. For generations, that premise appeared incontestable but, in the summer of 2007, it failed. It is clear that the levels of complexity to which market practitioners, at the height of their euphoria, carried risk-management techniques and risk-product design were too much for even the most sophisticated market players to handle prudently.

Even with the breakdown of self-regulation, the financial system would have held together had the second bulwark against crisis—our regulatory system—functioned effectively. But, under crisis pressure, it too failed. Only a year earlier, the Federal Deposit Insurance Corporation had noted that 'more than 99 per cent of all insured institutions met or exceeded the requirements of the highest regulatory capital standards'. US banks are extensively regulated and, even though our largest 10 to 15 banking institutions have had permanently assigned on-site examiners to oversee daily operations, many of these banks still took on toxic assets that brought them to their knees. The UK's heavily praised Financial Services Authority was unable to anticipate and prevent the bank run that threatened Northern Rock. The Basel Committee, representing regulatory authorities from the world's major financial systems, promulgated a set of capital rules that failed to foresee the need that arose in August 2007 for large capital buffers.

The important lesson is that bank regulators cannot fully or accurately forecast whether, for example, sub-prime mortgages will turn toxic, or a particular tranche of a collateralised debt obligation will default, or even if the financial system will seize up. A large fraction of such difficult forecasts will invariably be proved wrong.

What, in my experience, supervision and examination can do is set and enforce capital and collateral requirements and other rules that are preventative and do not require anticipating an uncertain future. It can, and has, put limits or prohibitions on certain types of bank lending, for example, in commercial real estate. But it is incumbent on advocates of new regulations that they improve the ability of financial institutions to direct a nation's savings into the most productive capital investments—those that enhance living standards. Much regulation fails that test and is often costly and counterproductive. Regulation should enhance the effectiveness of competitive markets, not impede them. Competition, not protectionism, is the source of capitalism's great success over the generations.

New regulatory challenges arise because of the recently proven fact that some financial institutions have become too big to fail as their failure would raise systemic concerns. This status gives them a highly market distorting special competitive advantage in pricing their debt and equities. The solution is to have graduated regulatory capital requirements to discourage them from becoming too big and to offset their competitive advantage. In any event, we need not rush to reform. Private markets are now imposing far greater restraint than would any of the current sets of regulatory proposals.

Free market capitalism has emerged from the battle of ideas as the most effective means to maximise material wellbeing, but it has also been periodically derailed by asset-price bubbles and rare but devastating economic collapse that engenders widespread misery. Bubbles seem to require prolonged periods of prosperity, damped inflation and low long-term interest rates. Euphoria-driven bubbles do not arise in inflation-racked or unsuccessful economies. I do not recall bubbles emerging in the former Soviet Union.

History also demonstrates that underpriced risk—the hallmark of bubbles—can persist for years. I feared 'irrational exuberance' in 1996, but the dotcom bubble proceeded to inflate for another four years. Similarly, I opined in a federal open market committee meeting in 2002 that 'it's hard to escape the conclusion that... our extraordinary housing boom...

financed by very large increases in mortgage debt, cannot continue indefinitely into the future'. The housing bubble did continue to inflate into 2006.

It has rarely been a problem of judging when risk is historically underpriced. Credit spreads are reliable guides. Anticipating the onset of crisis, however, appears out of our forecasting reach. Financial crises are defined by a sharp discontinuity of asset prices. But that requires that the crisis be largely unanticipated by market participants. For, were it otherwise, financial arbitrage would have diverted it. Earlier this decade, for example, it was widely expected that the next crisis would be triggered by the large and persistent US current-account deficit precipitating a collapse of the US dollar. The dollar accordingly came under heavy selling pressure. The rise in the euro-dollar exchange rate from, say, 1.10 in the spring of 2003 to 1.30 at the end of 2004 appears to have arbitraged away the presumed dollar trigger of the 'next' crisis. Instead, arguably, it was the excess securitisation of US sub-prime mortgages that unexpectedly set off the current solvency crisis.

Once a bubble emerges out of an exceptionally positive economic environment, an inbred propensity of human nature fosters speculative fever that builds on itself, seeking new unexplored, leveraged areas of profit. Mortgage-backed securities were sliced into collateralised debt obligations and then into CDOs squared. Speculative fever creates new avenues of excess until the house of cards collapses. What causes it finally to fall? Reality.

An event shocks markets when it contradicts conventional wisdom of how the financial world is supposed to work. The uncertainty leads to a dramatic disengagement by the financial community that almost always requires sales and, hence, lower prices of goods and assets. We can model the euphoria and the fear stage of the business cycle. Their parameters are quite different. We have never successfully modelled the transition from euphoria to fear.

I do not question that central banks can defuse any bubble. But it has been my experience that unless monetary policy crushes economic activity and, for example, breaks the back of rising profits or rents, policy actions to abort bubbles will fail. I know of no instance where incremental monetary policy has defused a bubble.

I believe that recent risk spreads suggest that markets require perhaps 13 or 14 per cent capital (up from 10 per cent) before US banks are likely to lend freely again. Thus, before we probe too deeply into what type of new regulatory structure is appropriate, we have to find ways to restore our broken system of financial intermediation.

Restoring the US banking system is a key requirement of global rebalancing. The US Treasury's purchase of $250 billion of preferred stock of US commercial banks under the troubled asset relief programme (subsequent to the Lehman Brothers default) was measurably successful in reducing the risk of US bank insolvency. But, starting in January this year, without further investments from the US Treasury, the improvement has stalled. The restoration of normal bank lending by banks will require a very large capital infusion from private or public sources. Analysis of the US consolidated bank balance sheet suggests a potential loss of at least $1,000 billion out of the more than $12,000 billion of US commercial bank assets at original book value.

Through the end of 2008, approximately $500 billion had been written off, leaving an additional $500 billion yet to be recognised. But funding the latter $500 billion will not be enough to foster normal lending if investors in the liabilities of banks require, as I suspect, an additional 3-4 percentage points of cushion in their equity capital-to-asset ratios. The overall need appears to be north of $850 billion.

Some is being replenished by increased bank cash flow. A turnaround of global equity prices could deliver a far larger part of those needs. Still, a deep hole must be filled, probably with sovereign US Treasury credits. It is too soon to evaluate the US Treasury's most recent public-private initiatives. Hopefully, they will succeed in removing much of the heavy burden of illiquid bank assets.

ADAM SMITH
NEVER STOOD ALONE

the pioneer of economics recognised the
limits of the free market 250 years ago

✹

AMARTYA SEN

Exactly 90 years ago, in March 1919, faced with another economic crisis, Vladimir Lenin discussed the dire straits of contemporary capitalism. He was, however, unwilling to write an epitaph: 'To believe that there is no way out of the present crisis for capitalism is an error.' That particular expectation of Lenin's, unlike some he held, proved to be correct enough. Even though American and European markets got into further problems in the 1920s, followed by the Great Depression of the 1930s, in the long haul after the end of the Second World War, the market economy has been exceptionally dynamic, generating unprecedented expansion of the global economy over the past 60 years. Not any more, at least not right now. The global economic crisis began suddenly in the American autumn and is gathering speed at a frightening rate, and government attempts to stop it have had very little success despite unprecedented commitments of public funds.

The question that arises most forcefully now is not so much about the end of capitalism as about the nature of capitalism and the need for change. The invoking of old and new capitalism played an energising part in the animated discussions that took place in the symposium on 'New World, New Capitalism' led by Nicolas Sarkozy, the French president, Tony Blair, the former British prime minister, and Angela Merkel, the German chancellor, in January in Paris.

The crisis, no matter how unbeatable it looks today, will eventually pass, but questions about future economic systems will remain. Do we really need a 'new capitalism', carrying, in some significant way, the capitalist banner, rather than a non-monolithic economic system that draws on a variety of institutions chosen pragmatically and values that we can defend with reason? Should we search for a new capitalism or for a 'new world'—to use the other term on offer at the Paris meeting—that need not take a specialised capitalist form? This is not only the question we face today, but I would argue it is also the question that the founder of modern economics, Adam Smith, in effect asked in the 18th century, even as he presented his pioneering analysis of the working of the market economy.

Smith never used the term capitalism (at least, so far as I have been able to trace), and it would also be hard to carve out from his works any theory of the sufficiency of the market economy, or of the need to accept the dominance of capital. He talked about the important role of broader values for the choice of behaviour, as well as the importance of institutions, in *The Wealth of Nations;* but it was in his first book, *The Theory of Moral Sentiments,* published exactly 250 years ago, that he extensively investigated the powerful role of non-profit values. While stating that 'prudence' was 'of all virtues that which is most helpful to the individual', Smith went on to argue that 'humanity, justice, generosity, and public spirit, are the qualities most useful to others'.

What exactly is capitalism? The standard definition seems to take reliance on markets for economic transactions as a necessary qualification for an economy to be seen as capitalist. In a similar way, dependence on the profit motive, and on individual entitlements based on private ownership, are seen as archetypal features of capitalism. However, if these are necessary requirements, are the economic systems we currently have, for example, in Europe and the US, genuinely capitalist?

All the affluent countries in the world—those in Europe, as well as the US, Canada, Japan, Singapore, South Korea, Taiwan, Australia and others—have depended for some time on transactions that occur largely outside the markets, such as unemployment benefits, public pensions and other features of social security, and the public provision of school education and healthcare. The creditable performance of the allegedly capitalist systems in the days when there were real achievements drew on a combination of institutions that went much beyond relying only on a profit-maximising market economy.

It is often overlooked that Smith did not take the pure market mechanism to be a free-standing performer of excellence, nor did he take the profit motive to be all that is needed. Perhaps the biggest mistake lies in interpreting Smith's limited discussion of why people seek trade as an exhaustive analysis of all the behavioural norms and institutions that he thought necessary for a market economy to work well. People seek trade because of self-interest—nothing more is needed, as Smith discussed in a statement that has been quoted again and again explaining why bakers, brewers, butchers and consumers seek trade.

However an economy needs other values and commitments such as mutual trust and confidence to work efficiently.

For example, Smith argued: 'When the people of any particular country has such confidence in the fortune, probity, and prudence of a particular banker, as to believe he is always ready to pay upon demand such of his promissory notes as are likely to be at any time presented to him; those notes come to have the same currency as gold and silver money, from the confidence that such money can at any time be had for them.'

Smith explained why this kind of trust does not always exist. Even though the champions of the baker-brewer-butcher reading of Smith enshrined in many economics books may be at a loss to understand the present crisis (people still have very good reason to seek more trade, only less opportunity), the far-reaching consequences of mistrust and lack of confidence in others, which have contributed to generating this crisis and are making a recovery so very difficult, would not have puzzled him.

There were, in fact, very good reasons for mistrust and the breakdown of assurance that contributed to the crisis today.

The obligations and responsibilities associated with transactions have in recent years become much harder to trace thanks to the rapid development of secondary markets involving derivatives and other financial instruments. This occurred at a time when the plentiful availability of credit, partly driven by the huge trading surpluses of some economies, most prominently China, magnified the scale of brash operations. A subprime lender who misled a borrower into taking unwise risks could pass off the financial instruments to other parties remote from the original transaction. The need for supervision and regulation has become much stronger over recent years. And yet the supervisory role of the government in the US in particular has been, over the same period, sharply curtailed, fed by an increasing belief in the self-regulatory nature of the market economy. Precisely as the need for state surveillance has grown, the provision of the needed supervision has shrunk.

This institutional vulnerability has implications not only for sharp practices, but also for a tendency towards over-speculation that, as Smith argued, tends to grip many human beings in their breathless search for profits. Smith called these promoters of excessive risk in search of profits 'prodigals and projectors'—which, by the way, is quite a good description of the entrepreneurs of subprime mortgages over the recent past.

The implicit faith in the wisdom of the standalone market economy, which is largely responsible for the removal of the established regulations in the US, tended to assume away the activities of prodigals and projectors in a way that would have shocked the pioneering exponent of the rationale of the market economy.

Despite all Smith did to explain and defend the constructive role of the market, he was deeply concerned about the incidence of poverty, illiteracy and relative deprivation that might remain despite a well-functioning market economy. He wanted institutional diversity and motivational variety, not monolithic markets and singular dominance of the profit motive. Smith was not only a defender of the role of the state in doing things the market might fail to do, such as universal education and poverty relief (he wanted greater freedom for the state-supported indigent than the Poor Laws of his day provided); he argued, in general, for institutional choices to fit the problems that arise rather than anchoring institutions to some fixed formula, such as leaving things to the market.

The economic difficulties of today do not, I would argue, call for some 'new capitalism', but they do demand an open-minded understanding of older ideas about the reach and limits of the market economy.

What is needed above all is a clear-headed appreciation of how different institutions work, along with an understanding of how a variety of organisations—from the market to the institutions of state—can together contribute to producing a more decent economic world.

GLOBALISATION
THE JEDI WAY

✳

SUBI RANGAN[3]

> *The Jedi are a 'noble order of protectors ... [that] hearken back to a more civilized, classical time in galactic history... As the Galactic Republic throve and grew over the centuries, the Jedi came to serve it as guardians of peace and justice.'*[4]

Humans have been engaged in long-distance trade for thousands of years. There is even some evidence of such trading from pre-Neolithic periods a few *tens* of thousands of years ago. No matter, today the development and dynamic that is globalisation conjures controversy and notoriety. There is a small but rising risk that if we don't come to better grips with the faults of the system called globalisation, we may be obliged to make messy corrections and even beat an untimely retreat. The human race has evolved on an impressive ability to learn. This does not mean that we make no mistakes; we often do and occasionally big ones.

Systems support and even produce actors. But actors' unrestrained actions may overburden and destroy the supportive system. If recent analysis and pronouncements are correct, this is the situation with global warming and related threats to our ecology, e.g. over-fishing. I would submit that globalisation risks inching up in that direction. I am not declaring that it is already there (or sounding an alarm bell) but I believe where there is smoke there is some fire. Fire keeps us warm, lets us cook and even wards off enemy predators, but we must tend to the fire lest the fire tends to us. I am going to argue that globalisation, like fire, is good, but 'JEDI' globalisation will keep the fire in the kitchen and burning longer than untrammelled globalisation. My arguments are simple and even basic. But in an advanced society neglect of the basics seems so often to be what gets us into trouble.

Under the system we refer to as globalisation actors and resources are obliged to relent to the forces of global supply and demand. Globalisation in essence increases competition and, influenced by information and communication technology, brings creeping contestability. Competition would appear to be a force (if not the most powerful force) for sustained, endogenous efficiency. Competition causes lower prices and in turn higher standards of real material well-being. Consumer welfare wins. Global (like local) competition follows this logic. Globalisation also means access to larger markets which, recalling Adam Smith, encourages greater specialisation. Specialisation also drives efficiency, not to mention quality. Last but not least, globalisation permits geographic diversification. This diversification reduces volatility of earnings and reduces business risk. Risk reduction is a good thing because volatility generally tends to hurt efficiency. Think of R&D projects that have to be abandoned because anticipated cash flows (from revenues) did not materialize because the economy took a dip or because of volatility in exchange rates. Stopping and starting R&D projects damages R&D productivity. The same is generally true for many other economic activities. Globalisation can help smoothen cash flows and reduce volatility through geographic diversification; if one economy is down, others may help compensate. Smooth cash flows are needed to support the productivity and efficiency of investment trajectories.

So if globalisation is such a good contributor to efficiency, what is the problem? There are in fact several, all well known although often discussed separately. Here I wish simply to highlight (what I perceive as) the important ones, and synthetically (if not logically) pull them together to suggest why business should aim for 'Jedi' globalisation over untrammelled globalisation.

Offer a reasonable person a choice between two values—efficiency and justice—and ask him or her, if they had to, to which value would they assign greater priority. (Before you read on, think of your own response.) In my unscientific survey (up and down my corridor, including some economists), as you might guess, justice won overwhelmingly. Efficiency is valuable and modern, but justice would seem precious and timeless. Globalisation has a truck with justice. Recall contestability. When workers elsewhere (say in another country) can perform a task more cost effectively than I can, then efficiency dictates that (i) either I improve my productivity in that task; or (ii) accept a cut in wages; or (iii) cede (exit?) that task or sector.

Improving productivity seems easier said than done. While wage increases are a norm, widespread or sharp (nominal) wage cuts are taboo. It is hence more efficient (faster, cheaper, less awkward) to shift jobs to the available cheaper new workers. But what if the incumbent workers' exit options are bleak? This raises a classic socioeconomic dilemma. Merit vs. need; efficiency vs. justice. Where does justice come in here? It comes in via the idea of implicit contracts. What are the implicit contracts of a business with its work force? It is silly to contend that there are none; only explicit contracts. Even in America where 'hire and fire' is the expectation, there are, or at least used to be, variations on this across firms (e.g., IBM in the East Coast vs. a startup 'tech firm' on the West Coast). If workers have made company-and-region-specific investments in their human capital, this will aid the firm. Some of this may be reflected in higher wages, but there generally is a component of deferred compensation (which was the implicit expectation of long-term employment). Few today expect a return to lifetime employment, but employees, especially given limited geographic mobility, are not wrong to invoke implicit contracts when they face abrupt plant closures or business relocations.

Justice is a big concept and I should clarify that I am plainly referring to distributive justice. Shouldn't there be more to it than bargaining skill and outside options when we decide my share and your share of the pie? In our current world of globalisation, capital and technology tend to be more mobile across regions and sectors than labour. Depending on the level and specificity of human capital, labour's outside options tend to be limited. If I wish to keep my job I have to take a steep wage cut; and if I take a job elsewhere I may have to relocate and often still take a wage cut. Is it fair that bargaining should be based on asymmetric relative mobility? Capital is more mobile so labour has to suck it up. This practice raises the question of whether firms are violating implicit contracts and acting unjustly. In such situations, where implicit expectations exist, labour may behave as if no loaf is better than half loaf. (Experiments in game theory yield steady evidence that unfairness puts the very game at risk. In the real world, the analogy would be in terms of eventual political implications.) Notice globalisation is not intentionally unjust, but if it unintentionally supports arguably unjust outcomes then the system builds discontents.

When workers exit and enter different sectors, the composition of a country's economy changes. This process is referred to as structural adjustment. Workers released in one sector are absorbed into another (with say temporary decline in wages). The absorbing sector may already exist or may be a new one (think of electronics in the 1970s; computers in the 1980s; biotechnology in the 1990s; renewable energy in the 2000s). Structural adjustment is good for global efficiency.

Such structural adjustment has been happening for more than a century, but in the 1980s and 1990s the pressure seems to have increased. More and more functions and industries are becoming 'contested' and, in light of recent trends (in software, back office functions, analysis, and even health care and advanced research), economists confess that it is hard to forecast which jobs/ functions (in services as well as manufacturing) are going to become contested. Technology is also shifting the comfortably predictable boundaries of tradeables and non-tradeables; there is growing contestability.

Liberal economists' main defence of globalisation today is that the net magnitudes of dislocations are small (i.e., dislocations are occurring but they are not widespread). This recalls one economist's thought-provoking quip, 'when you read that the unemployment rate is 5 per cent it does not mean that all of us are 5 percent unemployed, it means that 5 percent of us are 100 per cent unemployed.' Think also of the adage: better several guilty go free than even one innocent be punished. The question here is one of what is just?—rather than what is efficient.

In conventional discourse on globalisation, the above would be presented as a 'winners and losers' dilemma. But what I would like to emphasize is the expectations and the existence (or not) of complementary systems in society. If workers (such as in India, Japan, Europe) have implicit expectations that firms will not abruptly cut or cease activity in their region, then such cuts can be regarded as a breach of implicit contract to the extent of those expectations. This may harm the efficiency of an economy because trust is harmed and transactional exchange is encouraged.[5] In the long run if implicit contracts are breached all society may pay a price (not just the firms that do the breaching). Yes, expectations adjust, but in desirable ways?

The day before yesterday it was farmers, yesterday

it was manufacturing workers, today back office staff, and tomorrow it could be bankers, doctors, and teachers whose jobs are contested. I do not claim to have an easy answer. But what I do want to argue is that firms must comprehend and acknowledge their implicit contracts. If firms disregard the justice principle and focus solely on efficiency, then they are unintentionally making the system called globalisation fragile. Systems that are argued to be efficient but are unjust tend not to be sustained (e.g., slavery?). In the present case, the problem is compressed structural adjustment. For workers, cross-border geographic mobility is usually legally and socially unfeasible. This leaves sectoral mobility. In some societies, such as the United States, structural adjustment does work because the labour market was set up to be more flexible and complementary systems support mobility. In other societies, such as in continental Europe, the implicit contracts are different and complementary systems for structural adjustment function less well. It should then be understandable that protections are greater in Europe than in the United States. Bottom line: the pursuit of efficiency without justice will build a tenuous globalisation.

Business needs to convene with government to understand best practices in structural adjustment. How to make it attractive for emerging 'excess' workers to move to other sectors? How to improve their productivity in current occupations? How to encourage the creation of productive new sectors? This responsibility cannot be left to government.

Industrial policy is not governments' strength. Government understands taxes and transfers and (maybe) basic education, but (outside of fiscal and monetary policy) there is ample evidence all around that government has a much weaker understanding of job creation, entrepreneurship, and human capital upgrading. An understandable reaction from business might be that everybody is doing it. This response and neglect will, I fear, cause the system to eventually erode its legitimacy. Like global warming and Enron-type behaviour, business must be alert to the unintended ills of free-market capitalism and self-correct. Efficiency in globalisation must be preceded and supported by Justice.

In JEDI globalisation, I have discussed the J (justice) and the E (efficiency). I will briefly introduce the other two letters, D and I. The D here stands for diversity. From biodiversity to cultural diversity, to linguistic and intellectual diversity, there is good reason to preserve and revive it. Current best practices are 'best' under current circumstances. When the latter change, as they inevitably do, it is useful to have a repertoire of practices from which one might find a different practice that better addresses the new circumstance. A global seed bank inaugurated in Norway in 2008 is founded on this principle. It seems quixotic when France insists on a 'French way' as a counter to the 'American way' but there is sense in this. (One might ask whether the French are doing the right thing but for the wrong reasons. I happen to think the French insistence on maintaining variety is useful even if not seemingly short-run efficient.) The fallacy is that we take diversity for granted; in social settings—such as board rooms and cabinets—it actually requires investment and explicit cultivation.

Businesses now embrace diversity but often symbolically and out of political correctness. I would encourage business to regard diversity more seriously than as a compliance and image issue. Simply put, particularly on matters non-technical, business should resist using globalisation as a force to homogenize. This does not mean business is condemned to be local. But rather than imposing global, business has to learn to embrace *glocal*. Yes, JEDI globalisation may seem 'goldilocks' complicated. Sustainable human systems tend to be refined rather than crude.

The remaining letter in JEDI globalisation is I, which refers here to integrity. Is there integrity when I pursue global business just because there's a buck to be earned, even if the political and social systems in the regions where I do business are not savoury? Think of global business cosying up with dictators, despots and oppressive regimes to gain or maintain preferential access to resources or large markets. In those societies, local business has little choice; that's their institutional draw. But global business would appear to have greater choice. Exercising this choice will bring integrity to globalisation. Otherwise global business gives a bad name to the pursuit of efficiency and profits. The same goes for labour standards and environmental dumping. A sage statesman—Dr. A.P.J. Abdul Kalam, former president of India—

exhorted business executives recently to 'work with integrity, and succeed with integrity.' If in the case of globalisation without justice the point was that the ends should not supersede or displace other more important ends, globalisation without integrity is a case of where the ends don't justify the means.

In closing, my appeal is directed to business leaders. Think of justice, efficiency, diversity, and integrity (JEDI) as the four criteria that globalisation should meet if its present notoriety is to abate and if globalisation is to be sustainable. Recognize that whilst we have correctly crowned free-market capitalism as a superb economic innovation, we are still in early days as far as refinements go. It might mean that you will do less globalizing or go slower. Your actions and restraint today will make the system sustainable. Globalisation which promotes competition, specialisation, and diversification is a tremendous economic development of the last century. If we are to keep harvesting the efficiency crop of this great dynamic, it requires you to honour implicit and not only explicit contracts; revive and not only tolerate diversity; and operate at home and especially abroad with integrity.

May the Force be with you!

THE UK'S ROLE IN THE WORLD ECONOMY

✸

VINCENT CABLE

One of the few areas where there is a genuine all-party consensus is for Britain to have an open, liberal approach to trade and foreign investment and a positive attitude towards 'globalisation'. By contrast, in other major countries—the US, France, Germany, Italy, Japan, Russia, India, China, Brazil—there is fierce debate surrounding these issues. There are influential political figures, or even governments, arguing the case for economic nationalism and in some countries—notably the USA—there is a palpable sense of retreat from international economic integration. The current economic crisis is intensifying the pressures for nationalistic, beggar-my-neighbour solutions.[6] The UK does of course experience some dissent on the fringes—from Greens or the BNP—and there is a much broader unhappiness over large scale migration, but for the most part Britain remains one of the few *major* players unambiguously committed to an open economy and an international, rules-based economic system. This matters not just for the UK, narrowly, but because of its wider role in influencing EU commercial policy.

Britain's importance in the world economy is usually measured crudely in terms of its gross domestic product (GDP). In recent years this conventional measurement has shown the UK to have the world's fourth largest economy behind the US, Germany and Japan. This idea is a rather flattering one and, perhaps for this reason, has become a political cliché. The 'fact' is usually horribly mangled in the process; politicians often confuse GDP and GDP per head and so describe the UK as the 'fourth richest economy in the world', which is patently not true. Even the 'fact' is very misleading, reflecting the statistical benefits of what has been shown to have been a (temporarily) strong currency and the distorting effects of under-valued incomes in big, poor countries. The IMF and World Bank now use an adjusted 'purchasing power parity' measure of GDP which places Britain sixth (after China and India) and very close to France. Britain's advance up this league table in recent years (we were below France and Italy ten years ago) also obscures the important underlying trend that all developed countries are steadily shrinking in relative importance as China and India and other successful developing countries gradually reassert their dominance in the world economy which they enjoyed until roughly two centuries ago.[7] It remains to be seen whether British self-confidence in the global economy will be sustained through the current crisis as this shift becomes more apparent and concerns over 'economic security' are increasingly voiced.

The dominant 'free trade' orthodoxy which underlies the UK approach has its origins in arguments which were settled over 150 years ago.[8] There have since been attempts to overturn the orthodoxy, but these were unsuccessful and short-lived. Joseph Chamberlain tried to exploit economic nationalism at the turn of the 19th-20th century and came close to pulling the Conservatives with him. He appealed to the sense of insecurity that the world's then leading economy faced against new sources of competition.

Oswald Mosley's Fascists took up similar arguments, designed to appeal to working classes when threatened by 'cheap', 'sweated', foreign labour—particularly directed at the textile industry. However, despite the lack of competitiveness fostered by wartime 'self-sufficiency' and protected imperial markets, only the textile industry of the 1960s succeeded in winning any degree of tariff and trade quota protection in the post-war period. There was little traction in the flurry of industrial protectionism that accompanied the Labour left's 'alternative economic strategy' of the 1980s.[9] And there we remain.

It is possible that the current crisis will shatter the free trade consensus. There is intervention across Europe, the US, and elsewhere to protect politically sensitive major industries like vehicles by means of production subsidies. And it may become difficult to resist such pressure.

Another cloud on the horizon has been a certain amount of protectionist argument linked to environmentalism. There is a fashionable criticism of 'food miles', although it has been inconveniently pointed out that home grown, energy intensive food production may often be more environmentally damaging than food transported from the other side of the world. The most serious challenge in trade policy terms comes from manufacturing interests across the EU who claim that it is 'unfair' to have to compete against products from poor countries with lower environmental standards; a modern version of the 'sweated labour' argument and equally fallacious. By protecting energy intensive and relatively polluting industries like aluminium smelting against 'unfair' competition from even dirtier producers overseas, we create an incentive for our own sectors to specialise in relatively more energy intensive and polluting industries. And since the biggest environmental challenges, notably global warming, require global cooperation it is difficult to see how creating trade disputes with poor countries over precisely the same issues will help engender such cooperation.

But there is another challenge: 'economic security', particularly in relation to food and energy. The upsurge in world food prices last year gives a fillip to domestic producers who will noisily remind us of their importance, having quietly enjoyed produce prices well in excess of world prices for many years (or the subsidy equivalent). The recent panic over world food supplies produced a rash of export controls (alongside cuts in tariffs) across the world. But, in fact, the current crisis is a powerful reminder of why international agreement on trade liberalisation is so important since current shortages are caused in substantial part by the distorting effects of production subsidies (e.g. to bio fuels), past export subsidies and capricious use of import and export controls. There are techniques—strategic and buffer stocks, for example—for enhancing food security while preserving open markets. So far the British Government has been a helpful voice for sanity but it will need to be forceful in arguing the case within the EU. Unfortunately lack of agreement on this issue was one factor derailing the Doha Round trade regulations.

Global energy markets have been even more distorted and politicised. The OPEC cartel still functions. In almost all major producing countries outside North America, Australia and the UK, the oil (and gas) industry is dominated by state owned companies which pursue a mixture of commercial and politically driven objectives. Saudi Aramco, the Iranian National Oil Company, PDVSA, Remax, Gazprom, Sinopec, and other state companies mostly have financial and oil resources which far exceed those of the private oil 'majors'. It is these considerations which are leading the UK to pursue a new direction in long term energy supplies which relies less on 'free trade'—which would suggest a growing reliance on imported gas for power generation—and more on new domestic nuclear power. At present the Government is at pains to argue that nuclear power should be undertaken on a commercial basis with producers shouldering waste disposal as well as direct operating costs, but there will inevitably be protection, perhaps beyond a favourable 'carbon price'. Arguably the risks derived from importing gas are considerably exaggerated and can be reduced by diversifying supply sources and by strategic stocking, as already occurs for oil. But the main requirement is that the debate should be conducted on the basis of economic rationality, not nationalistic prejudices and insecurities which lead to bad decisions and all the costs of protectionism.

Where Britain has been exceptionally liberal is in

relation to direct foreign investment. Foreign companies now own the bulk of the electricity industry, the airports (BAA), water utilities, leading clearing banks (HSBC, Abbey) and investment banks, insurers, newspapers, much of what is left of large scale manufacturing—e.g. cars and steel—and leading football clubs. There are occasional grumbles (the performance of Ferrovial in running BAA) and some worries about potentially uncomfortable partners (Gazprom) but there is no concerted attempt to challenge the principle of foreign ownership in what were once seen as the 'commanding heights' of the UK economy. The 1970s provided the turning point for the current liberal foreign investment regime; the contraction of British manufacturing and the way Japanese producers turned the British car industry around put paid to most protectionist leanings.

For these reasons Britain has remained largely insulated from the current enthusiasm in France and, to a degree, Germany for 'national champions'. Similarly, despite a somewhat protectionist response to the 'threats' to imported gas supplies, there has been a very relaxed approach to foreign enterprises owning power stations and energy distribution companies. This is in marked contrast to the brittle nationalism demonstrated by the USA against foreign ownership of infrastructure, as seen with the threatened takeover of its ports by a Dubai group.

There are, however, still some awkward areas where the intellectual conviction that Britain is best served in a globalising economy by an open, competitive market clashes with nationalistic instincts, albeit usually expressed in the polite language of 'Great Britain Ltd'. The nearest Britain has to a 'national champion', in the French sense, is BAe Systems, the leading company in a substantial and generally profitable aerospace and arms industry. There are special factors operating here in as much as procurement for the armed services has an obvious—if often overstated—'strategic' dimension rather than a purely commercial one. Nonetheless there has been growing disillusionment with the costs, delays and quality limitations of a protected national supplier. The corruption and secrecy surrounding the vast Al Yammamah contracts with Saudi Arabia, and arms contracts in general, have inflicted considerable damage to the company's reputation and government determination to protect the commercial relationship with Saudi Arabia has seriously undermined the rule of law. But even this industry is yielding to the reality of international competition and the complex dealings of modern capitalism. A consortium with a strong French role, EADS, now plays a major role in big UK defence contracts. And BAe Systems is ceasing to be a British company, shifting its main base of operations and ownership to the USA.

Foreign direct investment is only one part of international capital flows, which are at the centre of what we call globalisation. Since the scrapping of exchange controls—almost two decades ago—the UK has been open to capital inflows and outflows. The City is now arguably the world's leading financial centre, hosting banking and other financial institutions which between them dominate some of the main international financial markets. Internationally traded financial services—the business of the City—now account for a substantial proportion of the economy[10] and taxation, via stamp duty on share transactions, taxation on incomes and capital gains and corporate tax. Indeed, until very recently London's dominance in the finance industry, central to the process of globalisation, seemed unassailable.

This certainty, however, has recently been called seriously into question, if not undermined. First, there is the fallout from the so-called 'credit crunch', the breakdown in inter-bank (and wider inter-institution) lending because of the lack of trust in hidden bad debts. In the UK, the crisis has exposed an awkward interface between the role of UK banks in international financial markets and their role as suppliers of liquidity to UK households and firms. The collapse of Northern Rock initially exposed this fault line, but the UK banking system as a whole is now struggling to re-establish access to liquidity and maintain credit flows. A leading global bank, RBS, whose balance sheet is bigger than the UK economy, has been effectively nationalised and others like Barclays depend ultimately on government guarantee. This same crisis has also exposed weaknesses in the UK system of regulation. 'Light touch' regulation, widely admired when introduced by the Financial Services Authority (FSA), turned out to be a crucial absence of supervision in the case of Northern Rock, HBOS and other institutions despite some prolific box-ticking. No-one at the FSA spotted the potential dangers of a reckless binge of lending at the peak of the market, backed by borrowing in international markets. The shape of the regulatory settlement that will follow this current crisis is not yet clear but it is bound to be less permissive.

A further problem is that it is increasingly difficult to separate the mores and incentives appropriate to a financial centre from those of the UK economy more generally. The City has been described, not altogether facetiously, as the world's first onshore tax haven. From the standpoint of the rest of the UK it sometimes appears similar to a mining enclave in a developing country, delivering a range of benefits to the economy but remote from the natives outside the fence. There has been a growing sense that the financial community earns obscene rewards, unrelated to risk or effort and seriously out of line with rewards in other sectors of the economy. The City is also seen to incubate tax avoidance loopholes, which are not available to other taxpayers. This was the mood which led to government proposals to tax 'non-domiciles' a flat rate sum. My own alternative is to welcome non-domiciles but for a maximum seven years after which they lose their privileged status. Either way, there is now an all-party consensus that no society can allow large numbers of its residents to operate, sometimes for more than one generation, outside the domestic tax system.

A more nationalistic approach to international

financial flows has been further fuelled by the emergence of Sovereign Wealth Funds (SWFs). These are the large publicly owned funds holding, and investing, the financial assets of mainly oil rich Middle Eastern, but also Chinese and other developing, countries. The models for these funds are the highly regarded and professionally run Norwegian and Singapore Funds. But there are apprehensions being expressed—notably in Germany and also in the USA—about what could be portrayed as nationalisation by foreign governments. In fact, almost all SWFs have so far endeavoured to invest in a non-political, professional way and they perform a valuable economic function in recycling surpluses back into the world economy. To their credit, the UK Government and the City have been rational and positive about SWFs but there are less rational demands elsewhere for controls over their flows. Beyond a legitimate expectation of transparency (over how much the Funds invest and where, and the governance arrangements), there is no reason to impose tougher controls on SWFs. Indeed, these funds could be a valuable source of new capital for the banks and other companies as the economy recovers. However, if the policy environment becomes more nationalistic in the EU, there will be strong pressures to move in that direction.

There is one respect in which Britain has partially retreated from global economic integration, with a move to tighter restrictions on immigration which has occurred in successive legislation and regulations since the early 1960s. Arguments about immigration policy are bedevilled by two major factual disagreements: about the scale of immigration and about the costs and benefits. As for the former, foreign-born people made up 9.7 per cent of the population in 2005, up from 6.7 per cent in 2003 and 3.6 per cent in 1993. The non-white ethnic population rose from 4.6 per cent in 1981 to 8.7 per cent in 2001 with a doubling of actual numbers, although a majority of the black population and over a third of the Asian population is UK born. These numbers are not exceptional by the standards of other comparable countries (8 per cent of the French population is foreign born, 13 per cent in the USA, 12.5 per cent in Sweden, 24 per cent in Australia and 13 per cent in Germany) and the ethnic minority population is close to 25 per cent in the USA.

There is, however, a wide gap between the actual numbers and the numbers as perceived by the host population. A recent survey suggests that the middle range estimates for the foreign population of the UK population was 25 per cent , over double the actual level, and a belief that the UK takes 20 per cent of the world's refugees as opposed to an actual 2 per cent . Further doubts have been created (and exaggerated) because of uncertainties in the estimates of net immigration since returning immigrants are not 'counted out' and there are an unknown number of illegals. What is not in doubt is that net inflows over the last decade have been at significantly higher levels than in earlier decades, averaging 160,000 as against minus 20,000 pa in the 1977-87 period and plus 20,000 in the

1987-97 period, much of the increase represented by Eastern European workers attracted to what was a growing economy but now has growing unemployment.

The debate about net benefits is also fraught with disagreements over facts as a recent House of Lords Report helpfully summarised.[11] There is broad agreement that immigration contributes to the economy by supplementing the labour force at a time of expansion and labour shortage, though the environment is now quite difficult with mounting unemployment. There is an argument too about whether living standards (per capita income) also rise. The net contribution to tax revenue and call on public services will depend heavily on whether immigrants are young workers or dependents. There are controversial debates too about the distributional effects, centring on whether the extra labour is competing with domestic labour or meeting hitherto unmet demand. The current UK position is characterised by a gradual tightening of restrictions, the effectiveness and appropriateness of which is often questionable. But in the face of rising unemployment it will be difficult to resist popular pressure for tighter controls. These, however, fall mainly on non-EU migration which is often crucial to maintaining business and job creation while East European migration, which is more acceptable with British workers, enjoys freedom of movement.

Looking forward, there are three major but unsettled questions about Britain's future role in the world economy. The first is over the relative importance of the UK. On current trends, the UK share of economic activity and world trade will decline steadily over time, not because of underperformance but because of the growing relative importance of the major new emerging economies. Second, the trend of the last sixty years has been for globalisation to increase the importance of world economic factors in the domestic economy e.g. trade, capital flows, migration. It should not be forgotten that a similar trend to ever deepening integration came to a brutal and destructive end in 1914 and it is conceivable that nationalistic forces could reassert themselves, particularly in relation to movements of people but also to trade and investment flows. The current crisis is putting that preposition to the test as never before. And, third, it is not clear whether Britain's integration with the world economy will occur through deeper integration within the EU or through liberalisation—and more rapid growth—outside the EU. In the past the two have gone together; the EU has not, as some pessimists predicted, become an inward looking 'fortress Europe'. Consequently the UK's commitment to strong global, multilateral institutions—notably the WTO—has broadly prevailed.[12] Hopefully, but not definitely, that will continue.

INVESTING IN THE UK vs INVESTING IN CHINA

rivals or partners?

✴

HAROLD CHEE

A burning question is why would any nation want to invest in a mature developed economy like the UK, when there are many other exciting new and virginal markets like Brazil, Russia, East Asian countries and others, with potentially higher returns? Received wisdom sees growing markets like China as a threat to mature markets like the UK. Yet in the context of globalisation it is naïve to understand the dynamics of the global market in the simplistic terms of countries like China sucking all the investment away from countries like the UK. The reality is that different markets are attractive to investors in different ways. In fact, we must rethink the nature of the relationship between mature and developing markets, and realise that the UK and China do not have to be rivals, but could sustain a mutually beneficial partnership.

As a mature market, the UK is attractive for certain kinds of investment, and there are several drivers for potential Chinese investment in the UK. On the flip side, there are considerable drivers for UK investment in the developing Chinese market. Perhaps it is a sign of the times that the Chinese New Year is now celebrated in the UK with all the fanfare and various cultural events to mark the occasion. Does this mark the beginning of good Sino-British business relations?

Since China's adoption of an 'open door' policy and the economic reforms begun in 1978, international trade and foreign direct investment (FDI) have played a key role in its rapid economic development, making it one of the fastest growing economies in the world. Its rapid economic growth and increased integration into the world economy, especially since the accession to the WTO in 2001, has increased China's share of world trade.

The UK is China's third largest trade partner and tops the EU for investment in China, with over 5,500 British invested projects in 2007. Some key reasons why many UK companies are eager to invest and set up operations in the Chinese market are: access to new market demand; low cost manufacture and labour which has led many UK companies to believe that it's the only way to remain competitive globally; sourcing of cheap products, components and raw materials; following existing MNC[13] customers as part of their supply chain; the 'learning laboratory'— China is where it's all happening and a market where UK firms can assess first-hand what their current and future competitors are doing and therefore adapt their strategies accordingly

Equally, there are many reasons why China presents a challenging business environment to UK, such as:

- No Intellectual Property Right (IPR) protection. Stories abound of many foreign companies having their processes and product designs copied without adequate protection and a weak legal system for compensation
- Although China has a potentially huge domestic market, the current levels of income distribution are unevenly distributed and skewed towards the urban sector

- China's huge labour supply is predominantly low skilled, and there is currently an acute shortage of middle to senior managers with the necessary competent level of experience in the industry, as well as an understanding of best practice globally in their field. Foreign companies are therefore finding it difficult to run their Chinese-based businesses effectively and efficiently. Because of the shortages of qualified management talent in the market, foreign firms are also finding that they have to pay very high levels of compensation to retain them, as job-hopping is quite common. This obviously increases the cost base and can be a major deterrent for UK companies to enter the market.

- The many logistical and bureaucratic hurdles facing the foreign investor, such as: the growing lengthy supply lines in China due to inadequate infrastructure, congestion on roads and ports, etc., which are forcing foreign companies to put their goods and stocks in warehouses, thereby increasing inventory and management costs; lack of transparency in procedures for example in mergers and acquisitions; state owned enterprises receiving preferential treatment, etc.

- Chinese business culture is a major barrier to investing in the market. There are so many horror stories of 'how not to succeed' in the market. Understanding the need to establish political and social connections, the meaning of 'face', 'guanxi' (relationships), and so on can be huge disincentives to engage in the Chinese market.

However, for UK companies that can manage the unfamiliar business terrain and culture, there are enormous opportunities in certain sectors. Currently, UK investment is focused in the following Chinese sectors: retail, telecommunications, financial services, energy and construction and infrastructure. However, there is still demand for British expertise in healthcare and education, utility companies such as water, niche high value-added manufacturers like aerospace, construction & chemicals, media companies, business services and leading global brand owners (given the Chinese propensity for rank and status in society).

China's outward investment is driven by four key determinants. The first is China's domestic situation, whereby Chinese multinational companies will seek outward investment because of capital market imperfections in the Chinese market. The Chinese government's 'Going Out' strategy is about encouraging Chinese companies to go abroad to seek new markets and resources. This strategy when coupled with financial support is giving them the added drive to seek outward investment.

The second is what we call market seeking FDI, where the goal is to find potential markets for its products and services. In addition to the domestic market situation explained above, Chinese companies are keen to expand their market share. To give added impetus to this drive, they face intense competition within the Chinese market from both international and domestic companies; and in addition, there is overcapacity in many sectors already, all of which are propelling Chinese firms to go abroad.

The third is natural resources seeking FDI, whereby China would look for the availability, quality and cost of raw materials and physical resources with an acceptable level of political risk. This means that although China needs enormous resources urgently to drive its engine of economic growth and sustain its development, it will not seek them at any cost. The Chinese approach in this context is what they would call win-win scenarios, whereby, the host country will benefit as much as China does. Take, for example, Africa—China is building roads, schools, hospitals, bridges, etc. in exchange for the raw materials it exports back to China. Chinese investments have exceeded over 9 billion dollars in 2007 in Africa alone, whereas the World Bank injected only 2.5 billion dollars into Africa in that year.

Finally, the fourth is strategic asset seeking FDI where China is seeking to invest in markets with technological, innovatory and other created assets (distribution channels, brands), as these would undoubtedly help it in gaining competitive advantages in the global market place. The Chinese are very keen to move away from the 'Made in China' label to the 'Invented in China'. This kind of investment would signal their coming of age by developing higher added value and higher quality products and services. This demands that Chinese companies learn western scientific and management technologies to better understand branding and business strategies in the global marketplace, and therefore increase their global awareness and market positions.

To facilitate its outward FDI, the Chinese established a sovereign wealth fund in 2007 (China Investment Corporation or CIC) to invest funds of US$200 billion of its huge foreign reserves of around 1.5 trillion dollars. Some commentators have said that this fund could triple in the next few years as China tries to move its foreign reserves out of low yield US treasury bonds.

Currently, Britain and China have a two way trade of around 30 billion dollars; Gordon Brown wants this to increase to 60 billion dollars by 2010. Chinese investment in the UK is small but the upside is that once the Chinese decide to focus their investment in the UK, their rate of growth is likely to be fast. Brown on a recent visit to China in Jan 2008 openly welcomed Chinese investment in the UK and said 'I want Britain to be the first location for Chinese investment, in Europe and the rest of the world.'

Brown's statement does infer some of the conditions for investing in the UK, which the Chinese might find attractive and fits in with their investment criteria. Certainly, the UK can be considered to be the gateway to the EU, the world's biggest single market, and Britain has a long tradition of doing business with all other European nations. This would be an attractive aspect of the UK for the Chinese who will no doubt see the potential of selling direct into the EU countries. London is perceived by many international companies as a centre for international business links; and well positioned for access to Europe, Africa and the Middle East. China's third largest oil company CNOOC said they will open their European headquarters in London shortly, because London is the global hub for oil and gas transactions. Furthermore, the UK's open trade environment and 'lighter' regulatory approach, say, when compared to the USA, makes the UK the preferred choice for investment.

Allied to this is the fact that English would be the language medium. Given that English is the de-facto business language in global markets, and with millions of Chinese taking English as their first choice foreign language, this is an added advantage for Chinese companies. One of the critical factors facing Sino-British enterprises is accessing a workforce with a high level of bilingual competence. In addition, for many Chinese firms with overseas aspirations, learning and communicating in English holds the key to success overseas. In fact, for many top Chinese executives, English proficiency is now a deciding factor as to whether their company can be a truly global organisation. The language factor makes investing in the UK an even more attractive prospect for Chinese companies.

Another market condition that would facilitate Chinese investment into the UK is the fact that London is a leading international financial centre and with relatively easy access to capital through the London Stock Exchange and the London Alternative Investment Market (AIM). This is an attractive factor for many Chinese companies, and some have already taken advantage of this access; one notable example is Hutchison China MediTech (Chi-Med), which is one of China's best-known suppliers of herbal medicines. Overall, there are over 40 Chinese companies now listed on the London Stock Exchange.

A key determinant mentioned earlier is the Chinese need for strategic investments. The Chinese would like to develop their technologies and own research base to move up the production value chain. For this to happen, China will need to invest internationally and this is where the UK offers enormous advantages. Britain is one of the leading countries for R&D in life sciences, computer and software services and renewable energy research. UK universities and research institutions are also comparatively very open and therefore an excellent base for collaboration on research, and this is where the UK can be an incentive for Chinese investments for the future. The paradox of China's economic success is the resulting environmental and pollution problems and the need to find alternative renewable energy resources. It has been estimated that China has already invested over 10 billion dollars in renewable energy capacity in 2007; this is second only to Germany. The Chinese will be looking to invest in sectors in the global market for these prioritised concerns. The UK is well placed here again to engage the Chinese on their concerns; for example, China has signed agreements with British Petroleum (BP) involving the development of clean energy technology.

In conclusion, there is a case to be made for investment in both developed mature economies like the UK, and in developing markets like China and India. Each sector has their own respective investment attractiveness. Perhaps it's not a case of companies investing all in one type of market, but diversifying their portfolio of investments globally. As for the UK, it has a tradition of open trade, a stable economic and political environment, a light touch regulatory environment when compared to its European partners, and extensive experience in the service industries such as finance, retaining, and utilities. These are all in high demand from emerging market countries like China. On the other hand, China offers enormous advantages to mature market investors like the UK; with an accelerating market for goods and services, outsourcing advantages and therefore gaining cost competitive advantages, access to highly skilled labour force such as engineers, science and computer graduates, and high returns on investments. It's time to stop seeing China just as a threat and embrace the opportunities it offers as a potential partner.

BRICS AND MORTAR

will brick economies be the future
foundation of
the world economy?

✸

JIM O'NEILL

It is now six and a half years since we first conceived of the BRICs acronym. On the back of the tragic events of 9/11, it dawned on me that in order for globalisation to continue, thrive and enable sustained advances, it was important for us to think of a changing world in which no one nation would necessarily dominate the future, and no one 'right' way of leading the world would be appropriate. In this spirit, I wrote an article entitled 'The World Needs Better Economic BRICs', which argued that in a world where important developing countries would continue to grow in size and stature, it will be crucial to re-organise the major global policymaking institutions. Six and a half years on, the need is even more urgent.

In 2003, Goldman Sachs (GS) first came out with our infamous 2050 projections. Using just two key long term economic variables, we showed that the combined GDP of Brazil, Russia, India and China could exceed that of the G6 (G7 minus Canada) by 2041. If you combine the likely working population and if every country achieved its productivity potential, then the BRICs projections would happen. However, it is important to remember that we never said that the BRICs 2050 projections will happen, only that they could. In reality, it would be quite surprising if all four BRIC economies achieved their potential at the same time. Some may get to their destination quicker, some may never get there.

In the past four years, we have repeatedly examined how the BRIC economies are progressing and whether any other large developing countries have the potential to be 'BRIC like'. If you consider the next eleven most populated developing countries—the 'N11' as we have dubbed them—only Mexico has the potential to be as big as any of the BRICs. To help monitor the ongoing progress of the BRICs (and other economies), in 2005 we developed an index of thirteen different variables, equally weighted, that are relevant for productivity—the Growth Environment Score (GES). Countries with a higher GES score are more likely to achieve their potential. When we updated our GES scores recently, China still has the highest amongst the BRICs, followed by Russia, Brazil and India respectively. The outlook for each individual BRIC as a future foundation of the global economy is very different.

Brazil

Of the four BRICs, Brazil is often regarded as the least deserving member. 'You only put Brazil in there because you needed the B' is a retort I hear often. But this attitude misunderstands what Brazil needs to do to be a competitive player in the global market.

It is true that Brazil has exhibited the weakest growth this decade, a mere 2.9 per cent . In our 2050 projections, we assumed that Brazil would grow by 3.5 per cent on average, and for this decade, 2000-2010, we assumed growth of just 3.1 per cent . Any observers expecting that Brazil can and should achieve China or India style 8-10 per cent growth rates are probably being naïve.

Why is Brazil in there then? 3.5 per cent growth over the long term isn't special. It boils down to how one defines a BRIC. Over the years, I have come to think the easiest way to assess a country's potential to be 'BRIC like' is whether it is big enough to be, individually, globally influential. Given that our 2050 projections show that Brazil's GDP could reach $8 trillion, eight times bigger than today, nearly matching Japan, and bigger than any single European country, it would seem to warrant the BRIC status.

Brazil has 170-180 million people, and importantly its demographic profile is highly favourable. Brazil may have closer to 250 million people by 2050, and the outlook for the size of its work force is considerably more vibrant than that of China or Russia.

With this favourable demographic outlook, why can Brazil not grow more quickly than 3.5 per cent ? 3.5 per cent for more than forty years would still deliver Brazil a lot. It could grow more, and indeed, in the 1960's and on many occasions since, 5 per cent was seen as a 'norm'. The most important thing that Brazil needs, however, is to 'avoid crisis' and to permanently rid itself of the hyper inflationary episodes of the 1980-2000 era. In this regard, sound macroeconomic policy making and at its core, Inflation Targeting (IT) by the central bank, is absolutely critical. If Brazil can succeed in creating an environment of low and stable inflation, it is quite likely this could lay the foundations for helping to achieve success in other areas of underachievement.

High real interest rates and relatively low domestic savings and investment rates have characterised Brazil since the late 1970s. A history of hyperinflation is not conducive to savings and investment. An environment of low and stable inflation would likely change this. In this regard, pessimists are undoubtedly underestimating the importance of the IT regime put in place in 1999. It is surely no coincidence that Brazil has avoided crisis since.

Brazil also has to raise the share of international trade and foreign direct investment (FDI) in its GDP. Looking at Brazil's GES scores, these are two key areas where Brazil underperforms the other BRIC economies. There is substantial evidence from past successful cases of economic development that achieving a significant share of international trade (and investment) appears to be a very positive catalyst. Brazil, blessed with abundant natural resources, especially ones in demand from China and Russia, has seen a notable improvement in its terms of trade. Using this temporary advantage to help bolster lasting improvements is important. Also, in this regard, the dramatic international focus on global warming and policies needed to combat climate change plays well for Brazil. Its early adoption of ethanol for environmentally-friendly energy can surely give Brazil an 'edge'.

In terms of overall GES scores, Brazil currently sits above India, but below China and Russia. On six of the thirteen variables Brazil scores more highly than the other BRICs, and relative to the N11, Brazil scores higher on nine of the thirteen variables that make up our GES scoring system. Consequently, Brazil seems to be 'reasonably' placed to deliver on our BRICs projections. It is probably not in a position to deliver growth comparable to China or India but to be a BRIC, it doesn't need to.

What needs to be understood by many people in the developed economies and of course, the developing world, is that there is quite a difference between size and wealth. While Brazil might not be capable of achieving the size of an India or a China, it is likely to maintain at least as comparable wealth to China, and considerably larger wealth than India. Our GDP estimates for 2050 in Brazil translate into average income of around $35,000 per head, more than double than that of India's.

Russia
Russia is typically regarded amongst GS clients as the second least justified member of the BRICs, but interestingly it scores notably above both Brazil and India in our GES scores.

Despite (or perhaps because of) Russia's poor demographic environment, our research shows that Russia has the potential to have a higher GDP per capita than the other BRICs, and controversially higher than all other European countries. If this materialises, it would open up all sorts of political and social issues for the EU and the world at large.

Russia's current demographic outlook is extremely poor with a projected decline in its population by more than 20 per cent by 2050, similar to the poorest demographically challenged G7 countries, Japan and Italy. Russia suffers from a low birth rate and a high death rate, and life expectancy for males is especially low. Very poor lifestyles and environmental issues dominate the weak life expectancy. Of course, it may be that improving wealth could raise life expectancy both by boosting birth rates and encouraging healthier lifestyles.

Two other areas are regarded as major problems for Russia: first, excessive reliance on energy resources for its wealth, and of course second, state control of many economic and social decisions, high private business and a lack of genuine freedom of choice for individuals. Yet Russia still has considerable economic potential.

Russia's GDP could grow to just under $6trillion by 2050 *if* everything went well, smaller than Brazil, but more than six times higher than today's levels.

To achieve its potential Russia would only need to grow by around 3.5 per cent, much lower than recent growth rates. If Russia repeats its growth performance of 2000-2005 it will become much larger than our GS BRICs projections. This is important to bear in mind in view of the 'gloom' about Russia's potential.

Russia could overtake Italy as soon as 2018, and each of France, the UK and ultimately Germany over the decade 2020 to 2030. Imagine Russia with a bigger economy than Germany? Not an impossibility within the next 25 years.

Looking at where Russia stands in the GS GES

index of 2005, it ranks at 81 out of 170 countries, about midway. Amongst a group of 133 developing countries, Russia would rank around 44th, i.e. *in the top third*. Relative to the other BRICs, Russia would rank a distant 2nd to China, but notably above both Brazil and India.

Of the variables, Russia ranks above the developing country mean for seven of them, three notably. Its macro-economic indicators, especially government and external deficits, rank favourably. It is of course arguable that high oil prices are giving such support that the strength of Russia's cyclical economic position is artificially positive. In terms of its fiscal position, Russia would currently rank the *highest* amongst all *large* developing countries.

If these macroeconomic scores artificially boost Russia's scores, the same is not true on education, where Russia is *significantly* above the performance of other big emerging market countries, both BRICs and so-called N11. Arguably, education is the single most important of the thirteen variables and maybe the most important when thinking about productivity. This powerful advantage should not be overlooked when considering Russia's future potential.

Compared to other developing countries with large populations, Russia also scores relatively high in terms of its usage of telephones, PCs and the internet. Together with the strength of its education system, this suggests that Russia is conceptually well placed to achieve its potential.

To get there, Russia needs to change, probably a

lot in terms of its weaknesses. In addition to its low life expectancy, concerns about political stability, the rule of law, corruption and the general creep of government into important aspects of everyday decision making, may justify scepticism.

These oft stated concerns might, however, exaggerate the negatives. Since the turn of the decade, Russian stocks have outperformed virtually all major markets including Brazil, India and China.

For Russia to achieve its BRICs potential, it almost definitely has to expand its economic prosperity beyond natural resources and, through other companies and businesses, to widen economic wealth ownership in its populace.

There are limited ways of achieving such an outcome, however. A highly attractive way for Russia to diversify away from its oil dependency would be to develop in two related areas:

Firstly, Russia could encourage foreign consumer multinationals. Keeping domestic ownership of the natural resource companies is perhaps not an illogical idea, but in terms of satisfying the rising aspirations of Russians, giving foreign companies good access to the domestic market makes more sense.

Secondly, Russia would be a desirable location for more producer-minded global market leaders in a number of industries seeking to export to the developing ex-Soviet States as well as possibly Iran, Iraq and other Middle Eastern nations, if such companies became more confident about the playing field in terms of international standards.

***

India

In the minds of many, India has the best potential of all the BRICs. India has over 1 billion people today, it has a much better demographic profile than China (as well as most other countries), it has a credible legal system and the English language is widely used. This is indeed why it is possible that India could overtake Japan in the next 30 years to become the third largest economy in the world. On a longer term horizon, India certainly has the potential to be the biggest.

However, looking at a GES type index, India is the lowest performing country of the BRICs group. In fact, India's outlook is riddled with contradictions.

India's natural advantages are large. Its demographic profile is very favourable, and its working age distribution is likely to remain very advantageous for decades ahead. India's relative outlook is potentially much better than the other BRICs.

Undoubtedly, the prospects for the size and relative growth of India's population are at the forefront of India's advantages. However, as many often say, what is so new? An analysis 50 years ago might have suggested similar optimism, and the fact is India never delivered. So why would it this time?

With its demographic riches, India has the potential for the economy to become fifty times larger than today. In fact, by 2050, India's labour force may be nearly as large as that of the combined labour force of China and the US. This offers absolutely enormous potential.

As sceptics argue though, potential is merely that—potential. Why has China done so much better than India? According to India's GES scores, it can be seen that investment, FDI and the literary rate are significantly below those of China. These factors, along with India's relatively closed economy, explain why China is the number one BRIC.

India is only ahead of the other large emerging market countries on 6 of the 13 criteria. On some indicators, especially the use of technology, India sits very low. Perhaps surprisingly, even when it comes to education, India is below the average of the biggest 15 population nations of the developing world.

Looking more closely at the educational issue, India does of course have a large number of well-trained, English-speaking technical graduates that are helping the country satisfy the demand for offshore services for the rest of the world. However, we must not exaggerate this benefit for India. In terms of the percentage of the population above the age of 15 receiving no schooling, India is significantly worse than all other BRIC countries. In 2000, 44 per cent of Indians aged over 15 received no schooling, more than double the number in China and Brazil and dramatically higher than Russia. UNESCO claims that the number of 'dropouts' in India in 2000-2001 was a disappointingly high 53 per cent . In this regard, the strength of India's educated workforce is something of a myth. Of course, given the quality of education in some areas, the potential for a large improvement in the numbers receiving a top class education is probably high, but big developments are necessary. Perhaps the ambition shown in the 2007 budget with respect to raising broad educational standards is a step in the right direction.

Of the other scores in the GES index, India scores very low in the technology and communications components. In terms of usage of PCs and the internet, India ranks below all except Bangladesh, Nigeria and Pakistan.

In terms of more macroeconomic factors, India scores poorly in terms of openness, with only Bangladesh and Pakistan below it. It is interesting in this regard that currently India has a balance of payments current account deficit, while the other BRICs have large surpluses. Indian imports are stronger than exports, and in addition, the combined total of exports and imports are very low for a country that has lots of potential to fulfil.

In some ways, perhaps India and China should swap places! China should reduce its share of GDP in trade, while India boost its.

India does have the potential to justify current optimism around the world investment markets but it needs to move more significantly in many key areas of reform in order to deliver the potential that is there.

China

China, the biggest economy in the world by 2035? This is what we often speculate. Many people think this means that China has to keep growing close to 10 per cent to get there. In fact, it only needs to grow by 5 per cent on average.

So what are the risks: bigger, sooner or later, or perhaps never? To get there sooner, China would have to grow by 10 per cent or more for the next 15 years, which is possible but unlikely.

It is distinctly possible that China will never get close to the size of the US. Economists, academics and journalists have made similar projections about other countries in the past. In the 1980s, especially when its currency was soaring, predictions of Japan taking over the number one slot early in the 21st century were rife but, ultimately, proven wrong.

China's current population gives it the potential to become the largest. However, this alone is clearly not sufficient. China needs to fulfil its potential by advancing its productivity performance and, just as with the other BRICs, it can only get there if it improves its microeconomic performance. It does already seem to be on the right road.

Our GES index places China second to Korea, with an average index value somewhat above those of the other BRICs. Amongst a list of 133 developing countries, including small ones, China comes a high 16th and some of its component scores are very high.

On macroeconomic indicators, China scores very well, close to 10 per cent for inflation stability, above 9.0 for its external financial position and high scores for investment and openness. Indeed, one wonders whether both investment and trade are too high a share of GDP for China's long term interests. This is an unusual dilemma. For most developing countries, the opposite problem is virtually always the challenge!

On nine of the 13 indicators in the GES index, China exceeds the average for the big developing countries and in reality there are only two where China is below the average: corruption and the use of PCs. Even in these two areas, China is not far below the mean.

Many different factors are thrown at China why it will fail. Usually among these, five issues are seen as key challenges for the country:

1. China will grow old before it grows prosperous.
2. Investment spending is too high and unprofitable.
3. China's rise in the past decade is based on cheap manufacturing exports, which is not sustainable.
4. China will not be able to control its people's wishes for Democracy and therefore civil unrest will result in chaos.
5. China will be able to control its people and therefore consumption will never take off, and eventually this will result in chaos!

There is no doubt that China faces similar challenges to many of the G7 countries, namely an ageing population and the threat of a declining labour force. Beyond the next decade, China could face similar challenges to much of developed Europe, especially those of Germany and France, although not quite as bad as Japan or Italy.

In this context, the next 15 years are perhaps really China's 'sweet spot' and, not surprisingly, GDP growth will lose the benefit of a rapidly expanding workforce. Without strong productivity improvements, China's growth surge will stop beyond the next 15 years or so.

It is not necessarily inevitable that China's working age population has to persistently decline. Two forces could improve the outlook. Firstly, rising wealth may encourage better health and social behaviour resulting in longer life expectancy and a desire for more children. Secondly, the government may respond to these desires by being more lax about enforcing the one child policy, or, of course, it could decide to deliberately relax the one child policy if it becomes concerned about the loss of human capital.

Compared to almost any other economy, the share of reported investment in China's GDP is high and, in coming years, it would seem highly desirable that private consumption should rise relative to investment.

There are, however, perhaps three different points which may question common 'wisdom' about China's investment being too high and unprofitable.

Firstly, many questions remain about the accuracy of reported Chinese official data. At the end of 2005, improved data showed that the overall economy was bigger by close to 10 per cent than previously thought and that investment spending was subsequently a smaller share of overall growth. It could easily still be the case that the data underestimates the size of services expenditure and the overall economy, and therefore still overstates the share of investment spending in GDP.

Secondly, there are significant doubts about how the official data for investment spending itself are estimated, and we suspect they are over-estimated.

Thirdly, much of the accusation about the unprofitability of China's investment spending originates in a very Anglo-Saxon type mentality. It is highly unlikely that Chinese policymakers or, for that matter, individuals would judge the 'profitability' of their investment spending over the same short term horizons that are commonly used in western financial markets. Given China's political and social structure, it is more likely that the 'success' of the investment build up in the past years can only be judged over the next decade or so.

While the surge in China's exports have both propelled China's growth and reflected the immense attraction of China's low wage advantage to many multinationals around the world, it has resulted in China having a large share of its economy in trade. Import growth has also risen dramatically to reflect both China's desire for commodities and other goods to help 'build' China, as well as imports for re-export from many other parts of Asia.

It is becoming increasingly difficult for the rest of the world to lose so much trade to China, and there is perhaps a growing risk of protection policies.

There are many US Congressional bodies monitoring China's export behaviour and its currency policy, and a continued rise in China's trade surplus will undoubtedly bring more pressures.

A closely related problem is that high dependency on exports increases a nation's vulnerability to other nations. China will face some significant challenges in the next couple of years if the US economy fulfils the worst of many people's fears and falls into recession.

Luckily, Chinese policymakers seem to be just as aware of this potential unfortunate outcome and they are preparing the population to shift more towards domestic demand leadership than overseas stimulus.

The ultimate 'problem' for China, especially in the minds of many investors is where and when China is going to become a democracy? Many observers believe that the longer it takes, the more likely it is that China could descend into disorganised chaos, while others believe that without democracy the economy will fail to 'deliver' causing chaos, and democracy will be sought to 'rescue' the country and its economy. Neither of these two extremes is likely to be right.

Given the vast diversity of China's geography, cultures and income groups, it is probably dangerous to envisage a world in the very near future where all 1.3 billion were allowed the degree of democratic freedom that many enjoy in the most developed societies. Undoubtedly, for China's BRIC like 'Dream' to come true of overtaking the US by 2035, by then its society will need to have changed a lot. How and when this occurs remain amongst the most fascinating and exciting challenges facing us all for the future.

GLOBALISATION

fostering inequality and poverty?

✳

CLARE SHORT[14]

'Poll reveals backlash in wealthy countries against globalisation' reported the Financial Times on 23 July 2007. It went on to summarise the poll findings: 'A popular backlash against globalisation and the leaders of the world's largest companies is sweeping all rich countries, an FT/Harris poll today shows.' According to the FT, the British in particular 'have the least admiration of any national group for the leaders of their country's largest companies, and a large majority believes the government should impose a pay cap on the heads of companies to limit their rewards.' It also claimed that large majorities of people in the US and across Europe are supportive of higher taxation for the rich to counter what they see as unjustified rewards. It continued:

> Believing that globalisation is an overwhelmingly negative force, citizens of rich countries are looking to governments to cushion the blows they perceive have come from liberalisation of their countries to trade with emerging countries.
>
> Those polled in the UK, France, the US and Spain were about three times more likely to say globalisation was having a negative rather than a positive effect on their countries.
>
> The depth of anti-globalisation feeling in the FT/Harris online poll, which surveyed more than 1000 people in each of the six countries, will dismay policy makers and corporate executives. Their view that opening economies

to free trade is beneficial to poor and rich countries alike is not shared by the citizens of rich countries.

These findings are important and interesting. Globalisation is frequently denounced as a cause of rising inequality within and between countries. This is not quite true—some countries, notably China, India and before them the East Asian tigers, have benefited greatly from the global flow of investment and trade. They are continuing to grow at higher rates that the OECD countries and therefore, by definition, the gap between these countries is narrowing. But there is growing inequality *within* these countries. And there is clear evidence that most of Africa, Central America and Central Asia are being left behind, leaving a billion people mired in poverty with their countries largely cut off from the global economy. Given that world population is authoritatively projected to grow to 8-9 billion by 2030-50 and that 90 per cent of the new people will live in the poorest countries, this exclusion of the bottom billion presents a great moral challenge and also a threat to the future safety and security of the world.

We must conclude that the overall economic growth in China and India and the increased economic growth in the OECD countries is not in fact 'lifting all boats'. Inequality within countries is growing across the world. The OECD's annual international employment outlook published in June 2007 said that 'a wedge had appeared between the rosy analysis put forward by economists and the much more sceptical view of the general public'. The report concluded that wages in OECD countries had, on the whole, been increasing in real terms, in spite of offshoring, but that globalisation could 'permanently increase' job insecurity for workers by making their employers more vulnerable to external shocks. Wages had in fact been shrinking as a proportion of national income in the US, Japan and Europe. Interestingly, earnings inequality had increased in all the countries for which figures were available, including Sweden and Norway but not in Ireland, Spain and Japan. The OECD suggested that globalised trade seemed to have made only a small contribution to increased inequality in recent decades but that technological changes might have a greater impact.

So, it is clear that recent times have seen not only a rise in poverty, but have created—in Galbraith's phrase—'a culture of contentment' where the majority do well and therefore vote against tax changes that would benefit the poor. Anger at rising inequality is spreading, and the insecurity of the present times is affecting the majority of people across the world.

Jeremy Warner, writing in *The Independent* on 23 June 2007, said he had gone back to his copy of *Das Kapital!* He explained this was not because he thought there would be a revival of revolutionary communism. Top down control had been tried and found wanting. Nor was it because the capitalist system has an inclination to repeated crises, which Marx thought would lead to its own destruction; developed economies have learned to manage their wild fluctuations. Instead:

> ... as Marx observed, part of the problem of entrepreneurially led growth of the type we are seeing today in particularly explosive form is that it creates social inequalities... the wealth gap between those at the top of society and those at the bottom is widening at a speed not seen since the days of nineteenth century cotton-barons.

The wealth creators of the industrial revolution find their parallel in today's private equity and hedge fund managers, and in the new breed of internet entrepreneurs. New industries and new companies are mushrooming, helping to create a separate class of super-wealthy. This in turn has generated a burgeoning service sector to cater for their needs.

One of the most striking features of today's global economy is the emergence of a cross-border super or cosmopolitan class. These people are more likely to have more in common with their counterparts on the other side of the world than they are with the less privileged members of their own societies.

The world's greatest cities provide the most vivid evidence of this new divide. In Mumbai, the super-rich live cheek by jowl with some of the poorest people on the planet—the £500,000 air conditioned apartment tumbles into a sea of slum dwellings with access to neither water nor electricity.

Even in more developed societies, the contrasts are scarcely less extreme, with the champagne lifestyle of London's super-rich played out against the backdrop of some of the worst sink estates in the land.

In the UK, inequality has grown and there has been a growth of poverty despite Gordon Brown's efforts to redistribute through tax credits. On 27 March 2007, official figures showed that the government was way off course in its ambition to halve the number of children living in households below the poverty line. In 2005/2006, 2.8 million children lived in poor households, an increase of 100,000 over 2004/2005. The Institute for Fiscal Studies said that the rise was in part the result of benefit and tax credit payments for some of the most vulnerable being increased more slowly than average incomes in 2005/2006. Increases were also modest in 2006/2007 and will be in 2007/2008 and IFS concluded that 'poverty may get worse before it gets better'.

The responsible Minister refused to commit to greater spending on benefits and said that a job offered the best route out of poverty. But the Joseph Rowntree Foundation report by Guy Palmer, Tom MacInnes and Peter Kenway, 'Monitoring Poverty and Social Exclusion' (first published in 2006) casts doubt on this assertion. It makes clear that half of the children still living in poverty are living in families doing paid work and conclude that 'the key proposition behind the government's strategy that "work is the route out of poverty" cannot be true for many people'. Unless the scale of in-work poverty can be reduced, future substantial reductions in child poverty are unlikely. This leaves the UK with 27 per cent of all its children in poverty, down from 33 per cent in 1998/1999. After 10 years of strong economic growth and a firm New Labour commitment to the reduction of child poverty, the reality remains that one third of British children are growing up in poverty.

Part of the explanation is the substantial problem of in-work poverty which has resulted in 6.2 million working age adults in poverty, more than pensioner and child poverty combined. More than half of these working adults do not have dependent children. Low pay is the major cause of in-work poverty.

On inequality, the Rowntree study finds that the income of the poorest tenth of households has gone up by 25 per cent, whilst that of the richest tenth has risen by 40 per cent. In proportional terms, levels of inequality are unchanged but, in money terms, the poorest decile have received a £10 a week increase and the top decile £320. As a result, three quarters of the increased income over the past decade has gone to households with above average incomes, and a third has gone to the richest tenth. This growth of inequality and poverty has been experienced despite Gordon Brown taking 5 per cent of net income from the richest 10 per cent of families to raise the income of the poorest by 12 per cent.

On top of this persistence of poverty and unequal distribution of the fruits of economic growth, Britain has become the country with the lowest social mobility of all the advanced countries. In 2005, the Sutton Trust published a study showing that there had been a sharp fall in cross generational mobility between those who were born in the 1960s and those who grew up in the 1980s. Another study by Stephen Machin's group at the London School of Economics, published in 2005, also found that the US and Britain were less mobile than other advanced countries. The UK was bottom of the league table. The strength of the relationship between educational attainment and family income, especially for access to higher education, is at the heart of Britain's low mobility culture. Norway has the greatest social mobility, followed by Denmark, Sweden and Finland.

And while the gap in opportunities between the rich and poor is similar in the US and UK, at least in the US it is static whereas in the UK it is getting wider. Depressingly, despite the big push to raise educational achievements since 1997, 27 per cent of 19 year olds in 2005/2006 lacked qualifications to NVQ2-level or equivalent. The Rowntree study concludes that 'substantial and sustained reductions in poverty in the long term depend on raising the level of qualifications among older teenagers and young adults in the bottom quarter of educational achievement'. The absence of progress here is a major concern for longer term progress on poverty reduction.

And thus we must conclude that globalisation is

leading to a growth of inequality and poverty in both rich and poor countries and to a complete marginalisation of the countries of the poorest billion. Britain is doing particularly badly, despite ambitious government commitments to a reduction in child poverty. In Asia, home to many economic miracles over the past few decades, the UN Millennium Development Goals Report 2007 indicated that income inequality is rising fast and the pace of poverty reduction slowing. It is difficult to judge the likely political effects of this in India and China but, back in the UK, the CBI Director General, Richard Lambert, said in a speech in London in July 2007 that 'unease about the widening inequality between top and bottom earners in Western society could fuel a political backlash against free market policies. Globalisation, technological advances and the new capitalism of private equity and hedge funds had created a general sense of insecurity and unfairness'.

The research evidence compiled by Richard Wilkinson is overwhelmingly clear: more unequal societies are more violent and crime ridden. Thus we now see, in most UK cities, armed drug gangs that have grown up at a time of unprecedented growth in prosperity. In a constituency like my own [Birmingham Ladywood], which takes in most of the central zone of Birmingham, Britain's second city, we have 20 per cent male unemployment, very poor housing—a problem exacerbated by the massive rise in house prices—a loss of well paid jobs in manufacturing thanks to globalisation, and a growth of low paid, insecure, service sector jobs. There have been some improvements in education and healthcare provision, but financial inequality is mirrored by gross inequalities in access to quality health services, and despite significant improvement in Birmingham schools the pressure to perform in constant tests leaves a large proportion of children alienated from the educational system.

Internationally, the poor of the world are urbanising very rapidly which will, I suspect, transform the politics of poverty as the poor of the world struggle to survive in squalid slums but are able to witness the pleasures of the globalised economy continuously on their TV screens. They are unlikely to remain as patient as previous generations of rural poor and will be in a position to protest, to riot and to organise politically as did British workers who lived in the slum cities of the industrial revolution.

The question is: will there be a political backlash? Will it lead to a growth in protectionism and a slowdown in this phase of globalisation? Will it create new political formations and a reinvention of social democracy, as we are seeing from the Scandinavians who are managing the change in the most civilised way? Will the poverty of the bottom billion conflate with the anger of the Muslim world? If we were wise, we would dedicate ourselves to distributing the fruits of economic growth more equitably and in preparing for the looming threat of climate change and environmental crises. As yet, there are few signs that we are wise, but perhaps it has to get worse before it gets better.

THE SOCIAL COST
OF ECONOMIC
GLOBALISATION

an indian perspective

✺

VANDANA SHIVA

Economic globalisation was heralded a decade ago as 'a rising tide that will raise all boats'. For the poor and vulnerable in the Third World it has been more like a tsunami, sweeping away what little security they had. Whilst economic globalisation impacts differently upon different societies and within different sections of those societies, it is the most vulnerable who are paying the highest price. In the case of Indian farmers, they are paying with their very lives.

Globalisation and Farmers' Suicides
Over the last 15 years, India's food and agriculture systems have been severely destabilized as a result of policies of economic globalisation and trade liberalisation. Two aspects of this destabilisation are the agrarian crisis and the rise in food prices, which have caused an epidemic of farmers' suicides and a rise in malnutrition. Anaemia has increased in women and children, and amongst the lowest 30 per cent of households the per capita calorie intake has fallen from 1830kcal in 1989 to 1600kcal in 1998, according to the national family health survey. In 1999-2000, almost 77 per cent of the rural population consumed less than the poverty line threshold of 2400kcal.

Farmers' suicides and the increase in malnutrition are related processes—both are the direct result of policies of corporate globalisation. This has led to:

- Increases in the costs of production
- Falling prices of farm produce

- Rising costs of food (a result of World Bank's Structural Adjustment Programme which has dismantled the PDS system[15], and of the weakened the Essential Commodities Act[16]).

Thus farmers earn less and the poor pay more. Produce prices fall while consumer prices rise.

The World Bank's 1991 Structural Adjustment Programme and the World Trade Organisation (WTO) rules that came into force in 1995 have jointly worked to dismantle the public framework for food sovereignty and food security. They have forced the integration of India's food and agricultural systems with the food and agricultural systems of rich countries.

The rise in food prices started as a result of India's domestic market being connected to global markets, especially through the imports of edible oil and wheat. In the early days of globalisation, the agribusinesses that dominate trade lowered prices to grab markets. This is what happened with the dumping of soya in the 1990s. Now that these global corporations (e.g. Cargill) have created import dependency, they are increasing prices. Price fixing is common practice amongst Multi-National Corporations (MNCs). The upward pressures on international prices are set to continue under the triple forces of speculation on futures trading, climate change and the increased demand for biofuels; especially as countries like Argentina, Ukraine and Russia have imposed export controls.

Under the 'globalisation, privatisation and liberalisation' agenda of the World Bank, WTO and International Monetary Fund (IMF), trade is more unfair than free. Structural adjustments have not removed centralised control over agriculture, but rather have concentrated it even further in the hands of agribusiness MNCs such as Monsanto, Cargill, Pepsico, etc. who are emerging as the new Zamindars.[17] Ultimately, it is the poorer sections in every society that are the losers. Over the years there has been an increasing asymmetry between world and domestic prices. Index numbers for Indian wholesale and consumer prices have more than doubled between 1990/91 and 1997/98, for almost all commodities. At the same time world commodity prices have been on the decline. The removal of import restrictions, as decreed by the World Bank reforms, has further increased India's exposure to global markets. As a result low international commodity prices, supported by high subsidies, are destroying domestic production and the livelihoods of the poor.

While the incomes of the poor go down, their expenditure is rising due to rising consumer prices. The growing gap between domestic consumer prices and international commodity prices refutes the claims by free trade propagandists that gains from unrestricted trade shall percolate down to consumers in the form of lower prices and higher quality. Corporations gain by low commodity prices while ordinary people lose with the rising costs of essential commodities. As Morisset has shown, the asymmetric response of domestic commodity prices to world prices is caused by the behaviour of international trading companies, not trade restrictions or bidding processing costs.[18] This has cost the commodity exporting countries over US$100 billion a year, by limiting the expansion of the final demand for these products in the major consumer markets.

So while consumers in India are paying more for their sustenance, at the macro level the country is getting less for what it exports, particularly in the face of a sharply declining currency value. Between 1980 and 1998 the non-fuel commodity price index declined by 45 per cent in constant prices, while by contrast the manufacturers' unit value index-I rose by 44 per cent over the same period of time. India's worsening trade deficit reflects these adverse trading terms, rising from Rs. 106 billion in 1990/91 to Rs. 345 billion in 1998/99.

At the same time as India was being made dependent on imports of food staples, Indian agriculture was being shifted to growing cash crops for export. Whilst banning the export of pulses and non-basmati rice, the government has prioritised the diversion of land to fruits, vegetables and cotton. This too has impacted on food security and self determination. Vegetables prices have gone up. Why is there a ban on the export of pulses and no ban on the export of vegetables? Is it because powerful countries like the USA want to control the pulse market, including selling to India? And will India continue its policy of being a supplier of cheap vegetables to rich consumers in the North whilst denying the poor in India food? Instead of decoupling the domestic food economy from the unstable, speculative global market, the government is strengthening the coupling, thus introducing major turbulence in both production and prices.

Neoliberal economist Bibek Debroy has welcomed the food crisis, saying 'the food crisis may finally catalyse agro reforms.... Liberalisation and integration bring domestic prices closer to global prices. Hence, Indian consumers will pay more for agro products, but pay less for manufactured products. That's the reform argument.'[19]

However, most poor Indians are earning less than Rs.20 per day and only spend on food—not on fridges and air-conditioning units. They can only lose with rising food prices. What economists like Debroy forget is that globalisation links prices, but wages grow more unequal. Rising prices with lower incomes for the poor translates into hunger and famine. While Debroy might celebrate the rising prices of food in India as the integration of our food economy with that of the corporate controlled world, the people of India are not celebrating. With 90 per cent of the incomes of the poor going on food, along with 45–55 per cent of the average Indian's income, it appears that the globalisation recipe does not work in a period of a global rise in food prices.

The solution to bringing food prices under

control and ending farmers' indebtedness and suicides are the same—the promotion of food sovereignty based on maximizing nutrition per acre while lowering input costs, as well as localising distribution chains.

Grow more wheat, sustainably
The Indian government is trying to project the rising prices of wheat as the result of low production and low productivity. The lowering of estimated wheat production from 73 metric tonnes to 68 metric tonnes was done at the behest of the United States Department of Agriculture and has been questioned by the Directorate of Wheat Research, which assessed production at 71-72 million tonnes. Of course, if the policy of importing wheat and shifting production from staple foods to vegetables and fruits for export continues, there will inevitably be a production crisis for food grains in the future. In the meantime, the government has proposed a package to 'grow more wheat', as if lack of domestic wheat production was the reason for the imports. However, the wheat package itself promotes increasing corporate control over our food supply. The Rs. 24.8 billion package has the following components:

- 'Seed Replacement'—meaning farmers giving up their tried and tested open pollinated varieties for hybrids and corporate seeds. It is in effect a corporate subsidy, not a subsidy to farmers.
- Subsidies for micro-nutrients, gypsum, sprinkler

sets and diesel, all of which are corporate subsidies not subsidies to farmers.

- Subsidising 'zero till' and 'conservation tillage' systems, which go hand in hand with the spread of corporate agricultural inputs.

The 'growing more wheat' package is also misplaced because instead of strengthening the sustainability of wheat production in wheat growing areas, it proposed promoting wheat in non-traditional areas such as Bihar and West Bengal which are rice growing regions.

Low seed replacement rate has been identified by the government as the main cause of low wheat productivity, along with the imbalanced use of fertilizers, high costs of inputs and depleting soil health. However, the package offered will further increase costs of inputs and deplete soil health because it is based on chemical rather than organic inputs.

Farmers' varieties are the best quality wheats in India. Compared to the 3.7 tonnes/ha that farmers are getting using high yielding varieties and chemicals, Navdanya's organic farmers in Uttar Pradesh are getting 6.2 tonnes/ha using native varieties. Navdanya's organic methods have increased productivity by 200 per cent . Instead of seed replacement we need seed conservation and participatory breeding by farmers; instead of micro-nutrients, gypsum and sprinkler irrigation we need organic manure which supplies micro-nutrients and conserves moisture; no till drill machines. Instead of subsidising corporations for non-renewable seeds and non-renewable inputs we need to support our small, local farmers to go organic.

The prionisation of culture

The influence of economic globalisation is not confined to our food and agricultural systems, but is felt at the most fundamental levels of society. Culture is the core of society—the embodiment of values and norms, of meaning and interpretation. It is a positive, lived experience. And as positive identity, cultural diversity can co-exist in peace. However, the stresses and pressures of globalisation change positive identities into negative identities; much like prions, the distorted proteins which were identified as causing the mad cow disease when cows were fed with the carcasses of diseased cows. Just as a prion becomes a self-infecting agent, the prionised cultures become self infecting agents in society.

The spread of economic globalisation has gone hand in hand with the rise of exclusivist philosophies and fundamentalist ideologies, both market and religious. These are underlined by the polarisation of identity. In Indian philosophy, we think in terms of *sohum*: 'you are, therefore I am'. Fundamentalisms, however, function on the belief 'if you are, I am not,' or 'my existence requires your annihilation'. Samuel Huntington's *Clash of Civilisations* is based on this paradigm of mutual exclusion, hence mutual annihilation: 'For peoples seeking identity and reinventing ethnicity, enemies are essential.'

As diverse cultures experience a threat to their values, norms and practices by globalisation, there is a cultural backlash. When the cultural response does not simultaneously defend economic democracy and create living economies, it takes the form of negative identities and negative cultures. As Amy Chua discusses in her book *World on Fire*, the economic polarisation of globalisation is superimposed upon existing class inequalities. These class inequalities frequently mirror ethnic patterns. Consequently class conflicts, she argues, often get camouflaged as ethnic conflicts.

The neoliberal ideology of development and globalisation wishes culture away, yet culture and economy are inseparable. Culture dominates and becomes the surrogate for concerns over livelihoods and economic security. Fundamentalist religion becomes, as Marx so aptly observed, an 'opiate of the masses.' The concrete context of culture—the food we eat, the clothes we wear, the languages we speak, the faiths we hold—is the source of our human identity. Economic globalisation has hijacked this, reducing it to a consumerist monoculture of McDonalds and Coca-Cola on the one hand, and negative identities of hate on the other.

Enduring peace and sustainability therefore require society to move to a paradigm beyond economic globalisation.

GLOBALISATION AND SMEs

opportunities and threats
for uk entrepreneurs

✺

PETER JONES

Businesses looking to create an international footprint have long been advised to 'think global, act local'. While this is undoubtedly a good guiding principle for formulating a multinational strategy, for entrepreneurs in start-up mode it is not likely to resonate much. With global brands such as HSBC and McDonalds it is clear that they are doing just this; HSBC's current TV advertising campaign has a very distinct global banking message; and McDonalds, of course, adapts its core menu depending upon local cultural influences—whilst the brand and the general proposition remain pretty much a constant no matter where you hunt down a Big Mac.

At the other end of the business scale, however, a new venture may well aspire to think globally and act locally, but the reality can be a steep hill to climb. International expansion takes up an enormous amount of resources in terms of both time and money. Understanding the local market demands solid on-the-ground knowledge and very often a physical presence and local employees—which in turn comes with its own maze of tax and legal issues to navigate. But as everyone knows, in the most basic form of international expansion the internet provides a very simple shop window to the world. Virtually every man and his dog can sell to the world these days, with eBay very much in the pioneering driving seat.

While you may be able to make a quick packet selling widgets from a web site, however, this is hardly likely to deliver long-term, sustainable growth, or indeed build a venture from which you can exit with a decent return on investment. It is important to recognise that entrepreneurs often only enter a business situation once they have a clear understanding of their exit point. With that in mind, one of the opportunities for a solidly performing, home-grown business is to get itself on the radar of an acquisitive global group, which may see it as a necessary addition to the corporate armoury. No matter what industry you operate in, it is worth understanding the main players—the big boys who are as much potential partners as they are competitors. Appreciating the global strategy of a company that might want to acquire yours can provide a wonderful exit route—but there are many hurdles to overcome before you get there.

If you have any ambitions to trade or develop internationally this should be enshrined in how you establish the business right from the off. Employ people with some international experience, either with work experience overseas or bi-lingual skills. Think about how the company is set up in terms of accounting and management principles, and make these as flexible to potential international growth as possible. But above all, have a clear strategy and plan that keeps you and the business focussed on how you are going to get there—and understand clearly why you are doing it. And when it comes to international expansion, lean on the agencies and bodies that can help to open doors—but be careful not to get bogged down in bureaucratic red tape.

The Department for Business, Enterprise and Regulatory Reform (DBERR)[20] has a wealth of support available for companies who fit its criteria for UK export growth. This ranges from basic country-by-country advice provided online and by a team of advisors to crucial grants and discounts for getting involved in trade delegations and international exhibition events. Business Links are a good starting point for tapping into these resources, or the DBERR website.

Some of the biggest potential threats to a business trading abroad are the cultural and language differences that exist—which can literally make or break a business. And even the bigger brands make mistakes.

There are some well documented examples of brands that translate into derisive or offensive terminology—which can be a real minefield, especially if you have laboured long and hard to find something that works in English and also invested in international Trademark fees. For example, Hershey's came up with the 'Cajeta Elegancita' candy bar. The Mexican term for caramel flavour made with goat's milk is 'cajeta'—so far, so good; but it is also a word for 'female genitalia' in Argentine slang, which, to put it mildly, did not transmit the desired message to consumers.

English into Spanish/Hispanic is a real treasure trove of examples—especially in the automotive industry. There are many lessons to be learned. When people chuckled at General Motors' Chevy Nova in Latin America, the automotive giant was perplexed. Until, that is, someone pointed out that 'Nova' means 'It doesn't go' in Spanish. Then there was the

Mitsubishi Pajero sport utility that caused embarrassment in Spain, where 'pajero' is slang for 'masturbator'. Toyota's Fiera car proved controversial in Puerto Rico, where 'fiera' translates to 'ugly old woman'.

Likewise few Germans were enthusiastic about owning Rolls-Royce's 'Silver Animal Droppings' car. To the English speaking world it bears the more romantic name 'Silver Mist'. And finally, Ford didn't have the reception they expected in Brazil when their 'Pinto' car flopped. Then they discovered that in Brazilian Portuguese slang, 'pinto' means 'small penis'.

So, it is clearly worth bearing in mind that your whole business can literally be lost in translation. When I founded my telecommunications firm back in 1998, I deliberately chose a name that would resonate within the global community: 'Phones International'. Such a title opens up the possibility for expansion right from the start. We in England are consistently fortunate that English has been the international language of business. However, with the emergence of the importance of the Chinese markets, this too could be changing, creating more linguistic hurdles for businesses to overcome. It's nevertheless an exciting environment for entrepreneurs who are 'thinking global'.

To conclude, the biggest threat to UK entrepreneurs is the lack of support and education that they are given at home. Before they can even begin to think on a global scale they need to understand basic business skills and terminology. Despite the hard work of several great business organisations, it is still difficult for entrepreneurs to know where and to whom to turn with their ideas, and this especially applies to young entrepreneurs. How do you get taken seriously at a young age? Who can provide that initial much-needed cash injection? And on top of these issues, entrepreneurs need to know how to register their businesses, understand patents, tax etc… all of which can seem daunting to the uninitiated.

As a nation, we ought to be encouraging creativity. Business needs to be taught in schools by businessmen themselves, by people who have been there and who understand the problems that entrepreneurs face. Our current educational system is not producing individuals who are ready to cope in the business world. Unlike our European counterparts, British students do not generally expect that their degree will be relevant to their career. This needs to be tackled, education needs to be made more modern and relevant, or as a nation, Britain will be left trailing behind the rest of Europe, and indeed the world.

BUSINESS AND SUSTAINABILITY

✸

STUART ROSE

Introduction

How can business reconcile sustainability with the need to be profitable? Isn't sustainability a 'nice to do' rather than a 'must do'?

These were questions put to me by the Industry and Parliament Trust in early discussions about this essay. I'm no Frederick Forsyth so I'm not going to attempt a 'cliffhanger'. Instead, I'm going to answer the Industry and Parliament Trust's questions at the outset by saying that for M&S sustainability is an absolute must if we are to be a successful 21st century business.

So what does the sustainability agenda look like for M&S? We're taking a lead on addressing what we believe are some of customers' most pressing concerns. Since the start of 2007, that lead has taken the form of Plan A, our £200m eco-plan. It has 100 action points but, at its simplest, comes down to five overall objectives we aim to meet by 2012.

By then, we aim to:

- Become carbon neutral while minimising offsetting;
- Send no waste to landfill from our operations;
- Extend sustainable sourcing of our raw materials;
- Set new standards in ethical trading;
- Help customers and M&S colleagues live a healthier lifestyle.

To fully understand Plan A, I believe it's necessary to understand its origins and potential impact. So why take a leadership position on sustainability? How was Plan A shaped? What impact has it had on our customers, our suppliers and our bottom line? As I write (September 2008), the economy is going into a downturn. Does this mean Plan A will fall by the wayside as purse-strings are tightened?

Why did M&S launch Plan A?
It could be argued that globalisation is behind the need for Plan A. After all, globalisation is inextricably linked to the likes of climate change and ethical trading. These are serious issues, and for M&S, doing nothing isn't an option. However I would say that globalisation and the issues associated with it are simply factors that play a part in the following reasons for adopting Plan A:

Firstly, Plan A is less than two years old, but it is in our genes. Our founding fathers were ahead of their time when it came to what they called 'enlightened self interest.' They believed, as we do now, that 'doing the right thing' is proper commercial behaviour, and ultimately leads to commercial success. They also believed in the need for continuous innovation. Plan A therefore is a natural continuation of these values in the 21st century.

Another key driver behind Plan A was our desire for differentiation. We deliberately wanted to, and could because we are an 'own brand' business, put clear blue water between ourselves and our rivals on the high street by launching a radical set of commitments which others would find hard to replicate.

We also believe that a public commitment like this brings us new opportunities to connect with our customers and employees. We know that the 21 million customers who come into our stores every week care about what we stand for, how we behave and what we are doing to earn their trust. Our employees feel just as passionately about this. M&S is what we call a 'taxi driver business'. No-one is short of an opinion about us, good or bad—whether it's where you stand on carrier bag charging, corporate governance or our food TV ads—all the subject of intense discussion on various blogs.

Before we launched Plan A, our customers told us they wanted government and businesses like M&S to take a lead and provide clear guidance on how they could get involved. This is something they expect us to do.

What's more, as a retailer we sit at a junction where we can really effect change. On the one hand we're linked into 2,000 suppliers, 20,000 farmers, 1,000s of raw material suppliers and a million workers from sectors as diverse as farming, chemicals, timber, food manufacture and plastics. On the other hand, millions of customers visit our stores in the 40 countries where we trade every week. This presents us with a huge management challenge—but also means that we have the chance to make a real impact.

What progress have we made?
20 months into Plan A and we're making good progress. 77 of our 100 Plan A actions are underway

and we've completed 14 of them. While there's still a long way to go to meet our targets, we are getting there. How have our customers—who are at the heart of everything we do—responded so far?

65 per cent of the people who shop at M&S would go green 'only if it's easy' or if we could 'show them the difference they could make.' This fact shaped Plan A. We are trying to make it as easy as possible for our customers to go green and show them that—even by acting individually—they can make a real difference.

Let me give you two examples:

First, charging 5p for food carrier bags. Since we started this in May, we've reduced customers' usage of carrier bags by 80 per cent, helping to cut plastic waste by saving over 100 million carrier bags from landfill. The 5p charge has also raised half a million pounds for Groundwork, an environmental charity. Carrier bag charging is not a panacea for all the world's ills, but it's also not a token gesture or a PR stunt. It's a good way of raising awareness of waste and landfill issues and how small steps can add up to something big.

Secondly, the Oxfam Clothing Exchange. Take your unwanted M&S clothes to Oxfam and get a £5 M&S voucher in return. We launched the initiative in January and it's already raised over £1m for Oxfam and stopped 1,000 tonnes of clothing going to landfill.

So we're making it simple for customers to 'go green' by providing them with easy to understand initiatives. We're also making it easier for customers to assess the carbon impact of their buying choices. We've introduced labelling on all our air freighted food products, and we're also contributing to the Carbon Trust and British Standards Institute's collaborative efforts to develop an effective carbon labeling scheme for consumer products and services.

Suppliers and Plan A
We are not only relying on our customers to make Plan A a success; we are also counting on the support of our suppliers. We have thousands of suppliers across the globe so can't deny that globalisation plays a large part in our business. We need to work effectively and efficiently with all these parties to build a sustainable business. It's a huge management challenge, reflecting multiple locations and cultures.

However Plan A is encouraging our suppliers to see environmental and social challenges less as an issue of basic compliance and more as an opportunity to innovate. They're bringing us ideas and solutions.

In turn, we're helping our suppliers in areas like sustainable construction and energy reduction. Take for example our 'green' supplier factories, opened in April 2008 in Sri Lanka. They incorporate a wealth of eco-features and are trialling a completely new approach to clothing production and setting standards for others to follow. The Brandix factory, which makes some of our casualwear ranges, is already delivering operational cost savings of £100,000 a year, while also setting new eco benchmarks. In addition, our lingerie factory in Sri Lanka is not only carbon neutral, uses 40 per cent less electricity and 50 per cent less water than a similar scale clothing factory, it also makes great quality underwear while ensuring its workers are treated well through leading standards in employee welfare.

Meanwhile, our Supplier Exchange website provides suppliers with information about our Plan A commitments and green best practice. More than 1,500 of our suppliers in over 30 countries have used the site. We can't get away from the fact that globalisation is here and here to stay, but what we can do is work with our global suppliers to encourage sustainability.

The commercial benefits of sustainability
We now know that Plan A is delivering. While we've a long way to go, it's already adding clear value to M&S as a business. It's engaged and motivated our employees who play a key role in delivering Plan A initiatives on the ground by, for example, encouraging customers to think twice about using new carrier bags each time they shop with us. They feel proud that we're continuing to assert Marks & Spencer's core value of 'doing the right thing'.

It's enhanced our brand reputation and is giving us the differentiation we were after—something that's very important in the intensely competitive retail sector. The research we've conducted with YouGov shows that when it comes to the environment, customers see us as being the UK's most caring major clothing and food retailer. Our store exit interviews with customers show the impact the launch of new initiatives—like Oxfam and carrier bag charging—have on customers' perceptions of our ethical stance. This is Plan A making a difference.

Cost savings and efficiency gains
When we first launched Plan A, we estimated the investment we'd need to make in the five year initiative would cost us around £200m. After only 20 months, Plan A is now cost neutral. The amount we're investing is balanced out by the amount we are saving through various initiatives.

The cost and efficiency gains that Plan A has delivered have been aided by our discovery of new ways of working—ones we would never have thought of before.

For example, before Plan A our store development teams and supply chain teams had never worked together. But our store development teams started work on a new generation of eco stores that save energy with more efficient heating, lighting and refrigeration systems. They then shared their expertise with our supply chain teams which have led to the new generation of eco-factories in Sri Lanka and also Wales which I referred to earlier.

The efficiencies and savings we're seeing from these new plants are invaluable and we're now looking at how we can apply them elsewhere, like in China. Any good retailer in today's world—with the consumer downturn, the rising cost of manufacture etc—is looking more than ever at their supply chain to deliver competitive advantage and help protect margins.

There are many other examples of how Plan A has made us look differently at how we operate and has brought us commercial and operational benefits as a result. One features the new low energy 20W lamps in our UK stores. These cost us £70 a unit, compared with £100 for the old-style lamps we were using. This one example of 'eco thinking' has not just saved us money but has also contributed to a reduction of CO2 emissions in our stores, offices, warehouses and delivery vehicles by nearly 50,000 tonnes, despite us opening 103 new stores.

There's another important commercial perspective to consider; the need to try and future-proof ourselves from the changing world. That means managing our business proactively, rather than waiting on the back foot for the world to manage us. As I write, rising fuel and energy prices, the increasing problem of waste disposal, scarcity of raw materials including water, and last but not least the likelihood of carbon charging, are all important issues for retailers as they impact the bottom line. Plan A has given us a secure platform to help our business respond to this changing world. It has given us the credibility, confidence and external networks to keep on the front foot.

The downturn

Now, onto the realities of the world we live in today. What impact has the consumer downturn had on Plan A? Market conditions now are very different from those back in January 2007 when we launched the programme and there's no doubt that consumers are feeling the pinch; this has made us more determined to forge ahead.

In fact, let me ask you, why would we ease back on cost saving green initiatives in a downturn? Doesn't it make more sense to accelerate them further?
Climate change won't slow down just because the economy does. The problems of waste, obesity, the depletion of the world's natural resources and poor working conditions in third world factories won't go away either. So, if we believe that doing our bit to tackle these issues is the right thing to do then we have to stick to our principles. Our customers have long memories—if we fold under the first sign of pressure they won't forget it.

Of course we need to adapt to what's going on around us. Initiatives like our Clothes Exchange with Oxfam are especially relevant to customers who are watching their pennies. And we need to stay sensitive to the fact that 'eco considerations' may not be such a high priority for our customers at the moment. Or we might need to convince them that 'going green' could actually save them money rather than cost them extra.

Conclusion
I hope that our own experience with Plan A will inspire others to adopt their own sustainability agenda and perhaps even take bold steps to adapt their organisations in a rapidly changing world. Why do I think others should be persuaded to do this? Because of the

many potential tangible and intangible benefits I now know they stand to gain. For M&S, Plan A is giving us a leadership position on sustainability and it's helping us stand apart from our competitors. Our new type of 'eco-thinking' is continuing to achieve significant cost savings whatever the economic climate. It means we can be on the front foot when it comes to being in tune with globalisation and how society and the world is changing, and we can make sense of what that means for our business, our customers, shareholders and suppliers.

Business leadership of the future has to involve sustainability. It's a necessity for any organisation that wants to succeed in the 21st century.

CORPORATE RESPONSIBILITY AND COMPETITIVENESS

✸

CHRIS TUPPEN

The globalisation of commerce is nothing new. All the great empires of the non-industrialised world engaged in widespread cross-boundary trade. But how this business was conducted was generally hidden from the end consumer. Although in some cases one can see the first glimmers of the dawn of ethical considerations. For example, in his book *The Corporation that Changed the World: How the East India Company Shaped the Modern Multinational*, Nick Robins describes how the significant power exercised by the East India Company gave rise to calls by Edmund Burke in 1783 for them to take a 'proportionable degree of responsibility'.

Adam Smith weighed in at the time with his *Inquiry into the Nature and Causes of the Wealth of Nations*, where he argued that over-mighty corporations were just as much the enemy of the open market as the over-mighty state. Not only did people pay for 'all the extraordinary profits which the company may have made', argued Smith, but they also suffered from 'all the extraordinary waste which the fraud and abuse, inseparable from the management of the affairs of so great a company, must necessarily have occasioned'.

One of the biggest differences between the eighteenth century and today is the instantaneous reach of global communications. This has not only fuelled the globalisation of commerce, to a point where it is actually quite a novelty now to purchase goods made or grown in one's local community, but has also been used by activists to bring companies to account for their actions across the globe.

As calls on business for more responsibility, accountability and transparency have grown, so too have the boundaries of expected influence. Today companies come under scrutiny concerning the working conditions in their supply chain, their employment practices, their use of outsourcing, the amounts and locations of the tax they pay, the carbon footprint of their operations and their products, and their role in alleviating poverty and disease in the developing world, to name but a few.

There was a time when many such matters sat fairly and squarely with governments and were expected to be overseen by the multilateral governance structures of the United Nations.

Take human rights—it is governments, not companies, that have formally signed up to the Universal Declaration of Human Rights (UDHR). Yet campaign groups have increasingly called on companies to explicitly state their support for the underlying principles encapsulated in the UDHR. These are wide-ranging and cover freedom of association, non-discrimination, abolition of slavery and forced labour, a fair wage, a safe work environment, liberty and security of the person, freedom from torture or cruel, inhuman or degrading treatment, peaceful assembly, freedom of thought, conscience and religion.

Large multi national companies became the focus of attention by the NGOs in part because there was no mechanism of redress at a country level and in part because of the influence the companies have (or at least are perceived to have) at a political and contractual level.

This matter came to a head in 2003, when the UN Commission on Human Rights tabled a set of Draft Norms on the Responsibilities of Transnational Corporations. The Draft Norms proposed mandatory reporting by companies, and periodic UN monitoring and verification of corporate compliance. International business groups vehemently opposed this approach on the basis that it was wrong to extend to private actors the same human rights responsibilities that bind governments under conventional international law.

It was left to John Ruggie, the UN Special Representative on Business and Human Rights, to find a pragmatic way forward. In 2008 he published *Protect, Respect and Remedy: a framework for business and human rights*. In it he concluded that the state has the principal duty to protect against human rights abuses, business has a corporate responsibility to respect human rights and the law should provide more effective access to remedies when things go wrong. He also said that 'Governments should not assume they are helping business by failing to provide adequate guidance for, or regulation of, the human rights impact of corporate activities. On the contrary, the less governments do the more they increase reputational and other risks to business'.

Calls on governments to provide clarity in such situations are not confined to the area of human rights. Through various organisations such as the World

Economic Forum, businesses have been increasingly calling on governments (and especially the G8 governments) to make clear and firm commitments around future action on climate change.

Since the industrial revolution, globalisation has been driven by a combination of free market economics, an international financial infrastructure, good transport links and the interconnectedness offered by electronic communications. Together these have delivered efficiencies of scale and, for the much of the world population, improved standards of living.

The climate change problem lies in the inexorable rise in greenhouse gas emissions as a result of the link between economic growth and energy consumption, to the extent that we have effectively exceeded the planet's natural capacity to contain the demand we place on its eco-systems.

There is now a dawning realisation of a real risk of the atmosphere going through a tipping point into what is termed 'catastrophic climate change'. If this happens it will result in major impacts on people, economies, biodiversity, food supply, national security and disease. A small number of entire countries may disappear altogether as sea levels rise. Climate change has been bred out of globalisation and represents one of the biggest tests ever of international collaboration and resolve. What the increasingly anxious scientists do tell us is that to avoid the worst happening we need to move with speed and determination towards a low carbon economy.

Dealing with these matters of corporate responsibility, or as many refer to them sustainability, is now a matter of market place competitiveness for both companies and countries.

At company level they drive competitiveness through:

- *Reputation*: building trust in a company is a long uphill climb, but losing it can have a dramatic effect on share price and customer loyalty.
- *Retention* and Recruitment: employees want to work for responsible companies who care for their workforce and contribute to society.
- *Operational Efficiency*: corporate responsibility can improve the bottom line through material efficiency, and energy and waste minimisation.
- *Increased Sales*: Cause related marketing, eco- and ethical labels and new product innovation can influence the top line.

This happens not by chance, but through a combination of well designed governance, strategic alignment with the company's market place and brand positioning, a motivated and properly skilled workforce and fully embedded ownership across the company's operations.

This is no small challenge—especially when there can be conflicting timeframes between short term commercial imperatives driven by dividend hungry investors and long term competitiveness. In their book *Built to Last: Successful Habits of Visionary Companies*, Collins and Poras found greatest longevity and commercial success amongst those companies that not only had a compelling vision but also stuck to a core ideology.

A number of companies have even found compelling links between customer satisfaction, employee motivation and corporate responsibility—all feeding off each other through a virtuous circle. But key to success is to keep corporate responsibility activities closely focussed around the company's core commercial propositions and not to be distracted into trying solve all the world's ills.

Philanthropy should be left to philanthropists; corporate responsibility should be based on delivering social and environmental benefit in ways that directly support the business.

But that's not to say there shouldn't be a strong sense of justice and ethics in what gets done. As Porritt and Tuppen say in *Just Values,* 'The business case for sustainable development won't work unless it generates real, lasting trust with all a company's principal stakeholders. And a company can't build trust on an amoral basis. Acting in more socially and environmentally responsible ways for purely instrumental, profit-maximising reasons threatens to undermine rather than build trust. You can't add value without values.'

As if this wasn't all complex enough, operating across the globe adds an extra dimension of challenge for companies who need to respect different cultures, widely varying levels of economic development and different views as to what corporate responsibility actually means. For example, in their 2005 survey Globescan asked the question 'what is the most important thing a company can do to be responsible?' The USA, Brazil, China, Argentina, France and Italy said to treat employees fairly; Canada, Great Britain, Australia and Indonesia said protect the environment; Germany said create jobs; and Russia, India and China said provide high quality, healthy and safe products.

Just like companies, countries also see themselves competing in the international market place. They want their industries to succeed and want their products to be purchased across the globe. In this respect country governments are also advised to encourage responsible corporate behaviour, especially as these matters are increasingly embedded in purchasing requirements in quite explicit ways. As Pascal Lamy, Director General of the World Trade Organisation has said 'Responsible Competitiveness is an essential ingredient for effective global markets. It blends forward-looking corporate strategies, innovative public policies, and a vibrant, engaged civil society. It is about creating a new generation of profitable products and business processes underpinned by rules that support societies' broader social, environmental and economic aims.'

Research in this area has been led by AccountAbility who regularly publish a Responsible Competitiveness Index The Index covers 108 countries accounting for 96 per cent of global economic activity, and blends 21 data streams from authoritative sources in assessing countries progress in advancing responsible business practices at the heart of their competitiveness strategies and practices.

The 2007 State of Responsible Competitiveness Index found Sweden as the world's most responsibly competitive nation, with Denmark, Finland, Iceland, the UK, Norway, New Zealand, Ireland, Australia, and Canada representing the rest of the top 10 in the index. Strong performers outside Europe include Chile, South Africa and the Republic of Korea. It is also interesting to see China adopting a much more supportive approach to responsible business and sustainable development.

According to Simon Zadek, CEO of AccountAbility 'Countries can compete responsibly and be successful, so long as governments and policy makers put in place the right frameworks. There needn't be a conflict between compassion and competitiveness.'

With careful attention globalisation, corporate responsibility and competitiveness can be welcome bedfellows. Together they could be used to deliver a more sustainable economy, but to do so they need the active participation of global business and all governments.

PROVIDING A GLOBAL TAX ENVIRONMENT

✸

JEFFREY OWEN

The global economy is in difficulty: a deepening financial crisis; record high food prices; a stalling of the Doha negotiations. In this environment it is crucial that governments identify and remove barriers to cross border trade and investment. Tax treaties play a key role in achieving this since they help prevent tax becoming the last trade barrier. We live in a world where multinational enterprises account for more than a third of cross-border activities, and where individuals and companies are increasingly footloose but tax administrations remain behind their national frontiers. There is a clear need for globally agreed rules on how to divide up the tax base between countries, how to eliminate double taxation and double non-taxation, and how to resolve cross-border tax disputes. The OECD Model Tax Convention, which this year celebrated its 50th anniversary, intends to meet these needs.

In September 2008, almost 700 senior tax officials and private sector representatives from 105 countries came together for two days at the Organisation for Economic Co-operation and Development (OECD) in Paris to celebrate the publication of the first draft of what was to become the *OECD Model Tax Convention on Income and on Capital*.

Over the past five decades the Model has served as the basis for the negotiation and application of bilateral tax treaties. A tax treaty is an international agreement concluded by countries for the avoidance of double taxation and the prevention of tax evasion. As such, tax treaties play a crucial role in removing tax-related barriers to cross-border trade and investment and in ensuring the full and fair enforcement of tax laws in a globalized economy. Fifty years ago there were only a few dozen such agreements in force between governments, but today there are more than 3,000 tax treaties, all based on the OECD Model. The Model also provides guidance on how these 3,000 treaties should be applied, and the courts—whether in the G7, BRICS or other countries—increasingly refer to these guidelines as the authoritative interpretation of bilateral tax treaties.

Bilateral tax treaties allocate taxing rights to countries and include other provisions which reduce the risk of double tax and include measures to reduce, and in some cases eliminate, withholding taxes on cross-border income flows. They also outlaw discriminatory taxes being applied to non-residents.

Treaties play an important role in combating offshore noncompliance, primarily by providing for the effective exchange of information between treaty partners. In a borderless world this role has taken on a new importance, and enables countries to count on the support of their treaty partners to help them in implementing their national tax laws.

From the perspective of business a key provision in treaties relates to the resolution of tax disputes, which inevitably arise in a modern complex economic environment: tax disputes between tax authorities as well as between tax authorities and taxpayers. In February 2008, the OECD issued a *25 Best Practices* to help improve what is called the *Mutual Agreement*

Procedure. The 2008 edition of the Model, which was issued in September 2008, takes this process one step further by providing a provision for mandatory arbitration whereby disputes which are not resolved within a 2-year period can be submitted to an arbitration panel.

Despite these successes the OECD is not complacent. It needs to streamline the procedures for updating the existing treaty network to take into account developments in the OECD Model, as it can currently take anywhere up to 15 years to get agreed changes into bilateral treaties. It is important that the OECD explores how it can develop a parallel Model for VAT. It is an aberration that, despite 141 countries having a VAT, there is no international consensus on some of the basic concepts of this tax and how it should be applied. The OECD also needs to strive harder for greater consistency in the application of treaties, both by OECD countries and non-OECD countries. Related to this, engagement with the BRICS, with the ASEAN countries and other non-OECD economies must deepen so that they have a louder voice at the OECD table. The OECD is pleased that in 2008 30 non-OECD countries have joined the 30 Member countries in formally setting out their position on the Model, but it needs to work harder at this engagement. The OECD also needs to follow very closely developments in the EU tax world to ensure that the work of the two organisations is complementary.

It is clear that the OECD has an important role to play in the future development of global taxation policy; we look forward to continuing to contribute to the development of truly globalised trade.

SOFT POWER AND AGGRESSIVE INVESTMENT

geopolitics and world trade

✸

ALAN DUNCAN

1989 proved to be a momentous year in international politics. On a chilly evening in November, we all sat glued to our television screens as the concrete symbol of what Winston Churchill had famously called the 'iron curtain' was torn down piece by piece. Euphoria spread through the Berlin streets. These were heady days for the West.

The swirl of events went to people's heads. America talked of victory over communism and freedom from oppression. It seemed that market forces had prevailed. One leading mind rather unwisely stuck his neck out and predicted the 'end of history', with the 'universalisation of Western liberal democracy as the final form of human government'.

This reaction is easy to mock in retrospect. The truth is that the Cold War weighed so heavily that its end was always going to be emotional. But the sense of triumph overawed the West's response to another event that also occurred in 1989, an event that proved (with hindsight) that Francis Fukuyama's vision would be short-lived.

This was the massacre of Tiananmen Square. Even though three years later Deng Xiaoping emerged from seclusion to continue the economic reforms he had initiated in 1979, the incident led to the retention of authoritarian rule in China and represented a significant setback to any major social reforms. More than anything, Tiananmen revealed that 'history' would continue its inexorable grind forward.

Almost 20 years on, the People's Republic of China is now set to become a—if not *the*—dominant global power of the 21st century. China's ability to be so lies in its size (1.3 billion citizens and climbing) and canny international networking—but most of all its capacity to trade. Last year, total Chinese trade reached $2.1 trillion, surpassing Germany as the second biggest trading nation in the world. China is at the centre of all the major new trade corridors that are emerging from advanced globalisation. Economically, it is breathing down America's neck.

So in one of history's ironies, the power of this communist regime and its ability to test and shape international politics has developed through precisely the same mechanism as that which finally destroyed its authoritarian peer in 1989: the free market. Just as the Soviet Union unravelled under the pressures of the fast developing world economy, China has been raised by it.

As such, rather than ushering in the idyllic new era of pluralism and democratic idealism that some desired, non-western countries have exploited the opportunities of globalisation and global trade to national, sometimes anti-western, advantage.

At the least, one of the features of today's global economy is that the rising powers—not just China, Russia and India, but Iran, Saudi Arabia, and Brazil too—have created entirely new corridors of trading activity that lie outside of western influence. This is visible within the crux of central Asian petro-states; throughout the Middle East; and across the traditionally western-dominated continent of Africa.

Moreover these developing nations, flush with

cash, are learning how to use their financial muscle to nudge aside the well established powers.

Over the last decade, for instance, China has been learning to use economic and trade strength not just as sticks but also as carrots—not only to overpower smaller nations, but also to woo them. In doing so, it is demonstrating how it is possible to outmanoeuvre the once indomitable United States.

In China's backyard in the Asia Pacific, where America has been the dominant power since 1945, China has been intensively seducing its neighbours and building support across the region. While Washington enforces sanctions (enforced on more countries throughout South-East Asia than any other region) and tightens restrictions on incoming visas, Beijing has opened up its coffers and its borders. By this year, 120,000 foreign students, many of them Asian, will have matriculated in China's universities, compared with just 8,000 in the early 1980s.

Africa has been another major focus of geopolitics and trade for China. Trade between the continent and China rose to $55 billion by the middle of 2006, which is a breathtaking 450 per cent increase from six years earlier. This makes Africa China's third largest trading region after the US and France. Alongside providing markets for its manufactured goods and tapping a rich source of energy, China also appears to delight in the political alliances that boast of its rising global influence.

And this influence is growing as fast as its apparent generosity. The latest 'action plan' provided a huge war chest to support 'reputable' Chinese firms across the continent, as well as agreements to double aid and pledges to establish schools (including the Chinese-language 'Confucius Institutes'), hospitals and health clinics.

So while Congress sits in Washington obsessing over the state of China's exports and the size of America's trade deficit, the People's Republic is carefully marketing its image as a hub of opportunity. One Chinese diplomat has been quoted as remarking that imports are the 'real diplomacy', 'because it means you're attractive to others. It means other countries need you, not that you need them'. This is a powerful point.

But it's not just China that is using its vast economic strength to geopolitical advantage. India is also learning to wield trade as a weapon of what is known as 'soft power', and no longer merely through its fine line in 'Bollywood' exports. As with several other fast developing powers, India has struck a rich seam with African trade, particularly in the west of the continent where expatriate Indians have traditionally chosen to settle. But in India's own region the interplay of politics and economics is particularly combustible.

Afghanistan is a particularly pertinent example of this for the UK. India and Pakistan have always historically vied for influence in Afghanistan, each attempting to outmanoeuvre the other. India, which supported the Northern Alliance against what they have formally and rightly described as five dark years of a 'reactionary, medieval and fundamentalist regime', is now pursuing greater engagement with Afghanistan. It is one of the leading benefactors of Afghanistan's reconstruction fund, having immediately donated about half a billion dollars following the Allied military action in 2001.

As is only to be expected, Pakistan has not reacted well to India's positioning—with its then leader Musharaff denouncing Indian consuls in Afghanistan as spy posts. This additional tension in Afghanistan's domestic affairs only piles further pressure on Hamid Karzai's already flimsy Government and has undermined the NATO mission.

A lifetime of visits to the Middle East and a brief but intense professional involvement in energy has given me first-hand experience of these deep sensitivies and the unrelenting tussling which lies at the heart of any trading.

But the most recent developments in global financial markets are particularly unsettling because they transcend physical ports and the packed hulks of cargo ships inching their way along the Persian coast, or trucks trekking their way across the mountainous borders of nation states. The real geopolitical future of trade in the 21st century is the instantaneous transaction across digital boundaries of vast sums of state money. This will be the era of the sovereign wealth fund (SWF).

SWFs have attracted an enormous amount of interest over the last few years, not all of it positive. This is for three central reasons.

First, the sheer scale of these funds would rattle

even the most composed economist. Around 30 countries have established funds (mainly sourced from oil and gas revenues or, in China's case, from the steady accumulation of US Treasury bonds) now worth an estimated $3 trillion. Even this figure seems puny compared to the staggering estimates of how much they'll be worth in 2015, which range from around $15–20 trillion. That's just under half of current global GDP.

Second, the vast majority of this cash belongs in financial structures that appear to wish to avoid any form of outside scrutiny. There is no publication of an investment strategy, no external auditing, no public accountability. The notable exception is Norway, whose fund works to certain prescribed ethical guidelines—a model of transparency.

Finally, there is concern in the west that these funds are being operated outside of the normal rules of financial markets—not purely for financial profit, but strategic gain. When western politicians see that the seven main players include Russia, China, Singapore and Abu Dhabi, their desire to address issues of transparency become increasingly urgent. At this point a mainly economic phenomenon becomes a political conundrum. Here we need to exercise particular caution in our response.

In reality, the concept of the sovereign fund has been around for some time. Kuwait's portfolio has been in existence since 1953—they have been a responsible shareholder in BP, Daimler and many other companies. But other countries have only just begun to make moves on the international money markets. Within the last year, state-owned companies have been demonstrating their financial capabilities. The Chinese-owned aluminium company Chinalco recently bought a 12 per cent stake in Rio Tinto and the Qatar-backed Delta Two was involved in an ill-fated takeover bid for Sainsbury's.

There are powerful political implications for western governments which conflict with traditional free market idealism. In January, Gordon Brown invited the China Investment Corporation to use London as a base for its operations, in exchange for opening up the Chinese economy to British services. Although it's absolutely right that free trade continues to be a priceless commodity, we must also act on two key concerns.

First, we have no idea how or if the Chinese will open their economy to our industries—there are currently strict limits on foreign ownership. And second, their investments in our businesses are irreversible even if the political climate worsens.

So we must always seek to gain more transparency in international markets. But our collective response to this should not be shrill. Recent moves by the European Union to establish a code for SWFs should be viewed with a certain degree of suspicion, given the protectionist instincts of some of its senior members. My own Party would be likely to react negatively if the UK was forced to adopt measures that stifled flows of investment. Similar proposals are being outlined in Washington and Canberra.

It is a particular kind of western hypocrisy that western firms who have been caught short by the credit crunch have been rescued by Chinese and Russian cash, only for their governments to suggest restricting future access to these same companies.

The old trading routes and relationships are changing at speed. Developing countries are deploying new and aggressive investment strategies. The sheer scale of the finance and the lack of transparency can raise the hairs on the back of politicians' necks. But we should remain aware that it is a collective advantage that trade continues to flow freely around the world. Although we must remain vigilant, it is in our best interests to continue to work within the international frameworks towards this goal.

DEMOGRAPHIC CHANGE, GLOBALISATION AND TRADE POLICY

✺

PETER MANDELSON

The problems of demographic change are quite different depending on whether you are looking at the developed or the developing world. Dramatic improvements in child survival and life expectancy have created a baby boom in the developing world that is projected to push the global population to nine billion by the middle of this century. According to the UN, 95 per cent of global population growth is taking place in the developing world, with the highest recorded growth in the Least Developed Countries. By contrast, in most industrialised countries populations are steady or even falling, with different policy implications. Growing and increasingly urbanised populations put serious strain on resources and the environment. They are a bulging workforce looking for work. Meanwhile slowing birth rates and aging workforces require managing pension policy and maintaining the economic resources to support a growing post-retirement population. The question here is how does economic globalisation affect the way we see these problems? And do these problems have implications for *trade* policy?

A billion new job-seekers
When we look at the links between demographic change and economic growth in the twentieth century we are led to some useful conclusions about trade policy and globalisation. Between 1950 and the end of the twentieth century, many states in Asia experienced a steep decline in infant mortality brought on by improved nutrition and healthcare. Although Asian

parents eventually responded to this dramatic improvement in infant survival by reducing birth rates, the delay between the mortality drop and the birth rate correction produced a 'baby-boom' generation. The result was that, in the three decades after 1965, Asia's working-age population bulged dramatically. The same advances in nutrition and healthcare that improve infant mortality and produce the baby boom also improve general longevity rates. So the baby boom generation also lives longer, as do subsequent generations. This is a pattern that has been repeated throughout Asia, including China, and Latin America. It is also evident in the countries of the southern Mediterranean rim.

In economic terms, the Asian baby boom posed a problem of excess labour supply. It injected millions of workers into economies that had relatively weak domestic demand and little employment beyond subsistence farming. Asian policymakers chose to solve part of this demand problem by progressively opening their economies to international trade. The resulting export-led growth provided an important outlet for the labour output of the Asian baby boom. This and the competitive stimulus of trade competition helped reinforce the dramatic growth rates that defined the Asian economic miracle.

The fact that all of the Asian economies were and are able to draw on a large pool of labour to fuel their dramatic economic growth is often used as part of the explanation for the Asian economic 'miracle'. This is undoubtedly the case. But in reality the Asian baby boom represented as much of a potential liability to the region as an asset. If this population bulge had not found sufficient employment if would have represented a ruinous drag on weak social welfare systems and even a potential source of serious social instability. The baby boom was not in itself the key to Asia's rapid growth. The key was the policy choices that enabled the population bulge to find work and accrue savings that were recycled back into the economy in the form of investment. This rising domestic demand ultimately balances the dependence on exports, although this balancing is still only in its earliest stages in economies like China's. Turning Asia's baby boom into an economic dividend required open trade policies that tapped the potential of global export markets and attracted investment.

This link between capturing the potential economic benefits of population growth and the right trade policy choices is reinforced by the experience of Latin America. These countries experienced a baby boom very similar to that in Asia, both at the same time and for the same reasons. But they have grown much more erratically over the same half-century. Whereas the Asian baby boom used international trade and globalisation to take up the slack in its working age population, Latin American policymakers tended to choose closed economies that could not generate sufficient employment for the huge cohort of workers moving through their populations. The increasing openness to globalisation in many Latin American countries is now beginning to correct this.

The countries of the southern Mediterranean basin now face a similar race to build economies fast enough to meet the needs of their growing populations—a serious regional stability challenge that should strongly engage the EU. The challenge for Sub-Saharan Africa is even more complex. Growing wage and production costs in Asia over the next two decades may present Sub-Saharan Africa with considerable opportunity to exploit a comparative advantage in labour costs and develop its own export-led boom. But taking advantage of this requires ending the scourge of endemic disease, fixing weak infrastructure and easing open some of the most ruinously protected markets in the global economy. We should be in little doubt that this will be the biggest development challenge of the current century.

So developing countries coping with a large demographic bulge face twin challenges. First, soaking up the labour surplus in an economically productive way. As a senior Egyptian policymaker said to me, when commenting on Egypt's 8 per cent growth rate in 2006, the Egyptian economy needs to grow that fast just to provide enough new jobs for a population that is growing at a net rate of a million new Egyptians every nine months. Export led growth, and the spur of inward trade and investment will have to be central to that growth.

Second, these countries need to plan for the point when that large baby boom generation reaches old age. Subsequent generations, relatively healthier and more prosperous, are already having fewer children.

This is a familiar problem in industrialised countries, but it is now also on the policy horizon of the first wave of Asian countries to globalise and industrialise after 1960. Savings rates in these economies already suggest that provision for retirement is a serious preoccupation for most wage earners, and this pattern is likely to reoccur throughout the developing world as countries industrialise and baby boomers age. The essential challenge for these economies therefore is to become rich before they get old.

Globalisation for the developing world's baby boomers
The implications for trade policy are important. The right economic policies make the difference between a generational population bulge that is an asset and one that is a liability. To capitalise on a large working age population an economy needs effective education systems to ensure that workers are literate and skilled. It needs labour market rules that enable companies to hire workers quickly and easily, and which protect workers as they move between jobs. However, the experience of the second half of the twentieth century also shows that there is a very clear link between a country's openness to globalisation and the extent to which it is able to capitalise economically on a growing population. Obviously, a long term development model cannot be built exclusively on export led growth—one of the major long term weaknesses in the Chinese model is its focus on export growth at the expense of developing domestic demand—but a degree of openness to globalisation is fundamental.

This openness is not simply a question of access to export markets. It can also be a question of access to vital imports, as the last year has shown. A rapidly growing population can put intense demands on domestic resources and for this reason many developing countries have become net importers of commodities. In some cases this demand can be met by improved local productivity, but in many case the only solution is to source from global markets. The recent food price crisis has reinforced how damaging it can be to food importers when countries erect barriers to farm exports in an attempt to secure domestic supply. These barriers cut off the very market signals that would push farmers to improve productivity. The net food importing countries, with their growing urban populations, now rely on a relatively open global market in agriculture to help encourage the supply to meet growing demand.

This is certainly not an argument for overnight liberalisation, and it does not suggest that free trade alone is the answer to poverty reduction in the developing world. There is no question that a policy of openness to trade needs to be flanked with other measures to help with the adjustment to open markets and the new pressures that they can put on workers. Open markets can spur economic growth, but societies also have to be equipped for the greater pace of economic change. There is a common assumption that 'development friendly' trade arrangements are those that provide developing countries with large amounts of flexibility to protect sensitive sectors or infant industry from trade. This is often important and necessary, especially to enable industries to reach the level where they can compete internationally or to protect subsistence farm livelihoods. However, the argument can easily be captured by vested economic interests or corrupt networks. No economy has ever taken the decisive step out of poverty from behind tariff walls. The cohort of emerging economies—China, India, Brazil and others—who have grown so quickly since the start of the 1990s have all been unilaterally liberalising their trade regimes for two decades.

So trade policy's most important response to demographic change should be to ensure that the openness of the global economy is maintained. We need to recognise the extent to which the openness of economies in Europe and the US is underwriting this push for development. The developed world's most important contribution to global poverty reduction in the second half of the twentieth century was not its aid or debt relief policies, but the openness of its markets. Without markets to sell into, there is no export-led growth. Supplying the demand of the developed world has been central to the Asian economic takeoff and is now underwriting growth in Latin America. The result has been the biggest rebalancing in global economic inequality in history. The fact that the west has benefited hugely from the same openness in terms of the competitive stimulus, growing markets for its own exports and access to cheaper imports and inputs, only reinforces its value.

The other potential engine for economic growth in

the developing world that remains significantly under-utilised is trade between developing countries themselves. Through its Economic Partnership Agreements with African, Caribbean and Pacific regions, the EU has used its trade policy to reinforce the development of regional markets. Although such regional market-building in Asia, Latin America, the Gulf and Africa is beginning to erode the trade barriers between developing countries, around three quarters of tariffs paid in the global economy are paid by one developing country to another. The most protected markets in the world are all in the developing world, most of them at the bottom of the development ladder. Although agricultural protectionism is usually regarded as the preserve of rich countries, farm protection in the rich world is far lower than it is in developing countries. This has inevitable costs in stalling the development of local and regional markets; it deprives companies of economies of scale and it acts as a disincentive for investment. The Doha round of world trade talks launched in 2001 was based on a development mandate that was interpreted by many simply as rich countries opening their markets to poorer ones. This has long strained credibility. If for no other reason than that the bulk of *new* demand in the global economy is being generated in developing countries, the question of freer trade *between* developing countries will only become more important.

The importance of investment and services
Looking for economic and trade responses to the

population bulge in the developing world can and should mean pushing the question of investment and trade in services to the centre of trade policy. Most developing countries initially have low capital stock and little scope for investment. Even with high domestic savings rates the money that will leverage the first big step out of poverty has to come from somewhere else. This is not a question of 'hot money'—it is the basic foreign direct investment formula applied globally with success that builds factories and creates jobs. If investors are not confident that their direct investment is secure they will locate somewhere else. The effect of this insecurity is all too apparent. Asia and parts of Latin America have been leveraging foreign investment for decades. Investment is now flowing into North Africa in growing amounts, which is vital for the region. But in Sub-Saharan Africa, inward investment rates are still low. African investors themselves are still choosing in huge numbers to invest outside of Africa. This will only be reversed by improving the level of confidence in the legal protection of investments and creating regulatory systems that offer predictability and transparency. It is not a question of the rich world pushing rules on poor countries. It is about agreeing common rules to enable the flow of foreign investment where it is most needed.

A similar development logic applies to the international trade in services such as banking, financial services, telecommunications, transport and construction. Investment by services companies in developing markets can be hugely beneficial, not only directly in terms of the jobs they create and the quality of services they supply, but also in the experience and skills that spill over into the local economy. Twenty years of working alongside and learning from British construction firms have helped Malaysian construction companies develop into some of the most competitive in Asia. Western banking and insurance companies bring expertise in financial management to China that Chinese managers are keen to acquire. Opening trade in services is not only the next frontier, but will be an important driver of the economic growth that will help create jobs for the baby boom in the developing world. Countries like India, with its formidable information technology and pharmaceutical industries are already advancing this agenda.

Services are also a key comparative advantage for the developed world and will be a trade policy priority. But the demographic situation of the developed world may strengthen the logic for freer global trade in services. A falling population means that access to labour and services provided by companies or workers from the developing world may fill an important gap in our own economies. Whether in terms of short term visiting workers providing domestic, hospitality or other specialist services, or in the remote provision of financial or business services, we are likely to find our own demographics strengthening the case for access to global services markets. The baby boom means there will be no shortage of willing providers.

***

A bigger slice of a bigger pie
A final general point about the implications of demographic change for trade policy applies to European businesses and governments. The rise of the emerging economies has exerted considerable pressure on some parts of European industry and there is an increase in zero-sum thinking about the economic consequences of the rise of Asia in particular. Yet Europe's trade surplus continues to grow and we remain highly competitive across a huge range of export sectors. Over the ten year period of India and China's dramatic rise, the EU has experienced a net job creation rate of more than 18 million jobs. While industries have had to adapt, and low cost manufacturing in Europe has continued to decline, the entry of three billion new people and perhaps one billion new workers into the global economy in the last twenty years has not cost us a single job on aggregate.

There are a number of reasons why this is the case, but among them is the simple fact that these growing economies are a huge new source of demand—the source of the bulk of *new* demand in the global economy—and European companies have on the whole positioned themselves well to exploit it. European market share in the global economy has remained stable over the last ten years, whereas that of the US and Japan has fallen. As the increasingly urbanised Asian baby boom attains middle class standards of living, it will constitute a huge new market for the high quality, sophisticated goods and services that Europe is good at producing. By the end of the decade the Chinese middle class population will be greater than France, Germany and Spain combined. It will spend around a trillion euros a year on consumer goods. The Indian economy is likely to generate similar levels of demand. The high levels of savings in these markets present a pool of capital and investment that is an opportunity for European companies. The growing Latin American middle class present a similar opportunity, with North Africa and the Gulf behind them.

Resisting protectionist pressure in Europe will mean making the case that Europe can either limit the openness of its markets thus capturing its domestic demand for itself, or it can maintain its openness and compete for a much bigger slice of the much larger pie created by growing demand in a global economy. We cannot have it both ways; closing our own markets from imports without facing similar barriers from others. Rather than trying to shut our economy off from competition, we should be focusing our trade policy and political energy on further opening markets in the fastest-growing economies for our goods and investment. In particular we should be helping Europe's small businesses equip themselves for export trade and be defending their interests in growing export markets.

Conclusion
It is not possible in such a short analysis to capture all the complexities of either demographic change or the

relationship between trade and development. But there is a central argument that holds true even at this general level: to turn a growing population in the developing world from a developmental liability into a development dividend requires rapid, sustainable economic growth. That economic growth is not possible without tapping progressively into the open markets created by globalisation. We in Europe can assist in this by underwriting open global markets; keeping our own markets open to developing country exports; helping developing countries build the capacity to integrate with the global economy through aid that targets infrastructure and business development; and encouraging developing countries to open their own markets to each other. Europeans should see the growth of these markets as an opportunity: as they become richer they will need more of what we make and sell. None of this is to minimise the problems raised by a growing global population. But we are better equipped to meet those problems with globalisation than without it.

NOTES

1. Research conducted on behalf of the Industry and Parliament Trust.
2. Brazil, Russia, India and China.
3. Discussions with Antonio Fatas, Landis Gabel, Philippe Laissus, Ilian Mihov, and Theo Vermaelen were helpful in shaping the substance of this essay.
4. From the Star Wars website http://www.starwars.com/databank/organisation/the-jediorder/
5. 'Transactional exchange' refers to a completely basic economic exchange, where there is no past or future to the buyer-seller (or employer-employee) relationship, and it exists only for the time it takes to perform a single transaction, so that no mutual trust or enduring relationship develops.
6. V Cable: *The Storm*, Atlantic Press, London, 2009.
7. Angus Maddison: *The World Economy: Historical Statistics*, 2004, OECD, Paris.
8. Described in D Irwin: *Against the Trade: An Intellectual History of Free Trade* 1996, Princeton University Press; and V Cable: *Protectionism and Industrial Decline* 1982, Hodder and Stoughton and Overseas Development Institute.
9. V Cable: *Import Controls: The Case Against*, 1978, Fabian Society.
10. 14 per cent of GDP is accounted for by financial services but it is not possible to separate out the traded part.
11. House of Lords Select Committee, 1st Report of Session 2007/8: *The Economic Impact of Immigration*.
12. V Cable: *Globalisation and Global Governance* 1999, Pinter and Chatham House.
13. MNC—multinational corporation.
14. This article was written in June 2007.
15. Public Distribution System, which ensures the distribution of essential items such as selected cereals, sugar and kerosene at subsidised prices to holders of ration cards.
16. The Essential Commodities Act 1955 was enacted to ensure easy availability of essential commodities to the consumers and to protect them from exploitation by unscrupulous traders through regulation and control of production, distribution and pricing.
17. Class who controlled the land and received rent on it during the time of the Mughal and British empires.
18. J Morriset: 'Unfair trade? Empirical evidence in world commodity markets over the past 25 years.' *World Bank Policy Research Working Paper No. 1815*, 1997.
19. Debroy, B. (2008) 'No time for field theories.' *Indian Express*.
20. Up until June 2007 was the Department for Trade and Industry (DTI).

INDUSTRY AND PARLIAMENT TRUST

Founded in 1977, the Industry and Parliament Trust (IPT) is a registered charity dedicated to promoting mutual understanding between the UK Parliament and the worlds of business, industry and commerce for the public benefit. This is achieved by encouraging dialogue between legislators and wealth generators from all sectors of business. The IPT is independent, non-partisan and non-lobbying.

Specifically, the IPT provides programmes of study, research, education and training in the organisation and practice of industry and commerce, and also of the administration of Government both within the United Kingdom and the European Union.

The following are the ways the IPT achieves its aim:

- Fellowships for MPs, MEPs, Peers and parliamentary officers; with the opportunity to spend time with one or more organisations in a range of industries. This enables parliamentarians to gain a greater understanding of the inner workings of business and enhance their appreciation of the impact of legislation on a company.

- Study Programmes and events for companies and organisations in the Houses of Parliament and in the European Institutions. These programmes offer participants insight into the mechanics of the legislative process, learning from those at the heart of political decision-making. Both our European Study Programme for Industry (ESPI) and our Parliamentary Study Programme for Industry (PSPI) are our flagship 4-day programmes which are held within the Houses of Parliament and EU Parliament Buildings in Brussels respectively.

- Attachment Schemes for civil servants, enabling them to see the parliamentary process at first hand in the company of an MP or MEP.

Sally Muggeridge
Chief Executive

Industry and Parliament Trust
Suite 101
3 Whitehall Court
London SW1A 2EL
United Kingdom

+44 (0)20 7839 9400 (tel)
+44 (0)20 7839 9401 (fax)
www.ipt.org.uk

SPONSORS* OF THE INDUSTRY AND PARLIAMENT TRUST

3M UK Plc

Aberdeen Asset Management Plc
Aggregate Industries Plc
Alliance Boots Plc
Alternative Investment Management
    Association Ltd
Anglo American Plc
The Argyll Consultancies
ARM Ltd
Arts Council England
Arup Group Ltd

BAE Systems Plc
Bank of America Securities Ltd
The Bank of England
Barclays Plc
BASF Plc
Bayer Schering Pharma
BP Marsh & Partners Ltd
BP Plc
British American Tobacco
    (Holdings) Ltd
British Broadcasting Corporation
British Telecommunications Plc

Britvic Soft Drinks Ltd

Cadbury Plc
Canon (UK) Ltd
The Carbon Neutral Company
Chiumento Consulting Ltd
Compass Group UK & Ireland Ltd
ConocoPhillips (UK) Ltd
The Co-operative Group

Degussa UK Holdings Ltd
DHL International Ltd

EA Technology
Electronic Data Systems Ltd
Energy Retail Association
ExxonMobil

Federation of Ophthalmic and
    Dispensing Opticians
The Federation of Small Businesses
Finmeccanica UK

Gallaher Ltd
GKN Plc

* The views expressed in this book are those of the contributors only.

GlaxoSmithKline UK Ltd
The Go-Ahead Group Plc

HR Insight Ltd

IDIS
Imperial College London
Imperial Tobacco Ltd
Irwin Mitchell
ITN Plc
ITV Plc

John Lewis Partnership
Johnson & Johnson
Judge Business School, Cambridge University

Kalyx Ltd
KPMG LLP

Ladbrokes Ltd
The Linde Group Plc
Lloyd's of London
Lloyds TSB Bank Plc
London Luton Airport Operations Ltd

The Maersk Company Ltd
Manchester Airports Group
Marks and Spencer Plc
Marsh Ltd
Motorola Ltd
MND Exploration & Production Ltd
Muncaster Visitors Management Ltd

Nestlé UK Ltd
Network Rail Infrastructure Ltd
The Noise Abatement Society
Nominet
Nuclear Decommissioning Authority

Pfizer Ltd

Pilkington Plc
Pineapple Developments Ltd
PricewaterhouseCoopers LLP
The Publishers' Association

Reed Elsevier (UK) Ltd
Rexam Plc
Rio Tinto Plc
Rolls-Royce PLC
Royal Armouries
The Royal Bank of Scotland Plc
Royal Holloway University of London
RWE Npower

Savills Hepher Dixon
Schering-Plough Ltd
Shell International Ltd
Short Brothers Plc
Smiths Group Plc
The Standard Life Assurance Company
StatOil (UK) Ltd

T-Mobile
Tesco Stores Ltd
Thales Plc
Thomas H Loveday Ltd
Throgmorton
TNT Post
Total Holdings UK Ltd
Transport for London
Tunstall Group Plc

Unilever UK Ltd
United Utilities Plc
Universities UK
University of Bristol
UPS Ltd

Waste Recycling Group Ltd